GRADE 6

Reader's and Writer's JOURNAL

SAVVAS
LEARNING COMPANY

Savvas Learning Company LLC, 15 East Midland Avenue, Paramus, NJ 07652

SAVVAS
LEARNING COMPANY

ISBN-13: 978-0-328-85161-4
ISBN-10: 0-328-85161-2
1 2 3 4 5 6 7 8 9 10 V0N4 19 18 17 16 15

9 2021

Table of Contents

Name ____________________

Benchmark Vocabulary

DIRECTIONS Write a sentence using each word.

deadpan cultivated showboating

Write in Response to Reading

Reread pages 18–21 of *The Egypt Game*. In this scene, the narrator uses only April's perspective as she talks with the Professor. Write a paragraph to explain how the narrator uses this point of view to reveal April's character and create suspense in the story. Find evidence in the text to support your ideas. Write your paragraph below or on a separate sheet of paper.

Students demonstrate contextual understanding of Benchmark Vocabulary. Students read text closely and use text evidence in their written answers.

Name ____________________

Writing

Narrative Writing: Establish Point of View Use your narrative planning ideas and notes to write a one-page introduction to a mystery. Remember that a good beginning for a story engages the reader's interest, orients the reader to the world of the story, and establishes a point of view. Make sure your introduction tells the reader about the setting, introduces the narrator and main character(s), and hints at the main problem in the mystery. Write your introduction on a separate sheet of paper or start a new document.

Conventions

Common, Proper, and Possessive Nouns

DIRECTIONS On the lines provided, write the proper or common nouns that should be capitalized in each sentence.

1. people often travel to exotic places such as the himalayas or the andes mountains.

   ____

2. I photographed washington square, grand central station, and three other historic buildings.

   ____

3. Why is renee taking orchard street when this street is so much shorter?

   ____

DIRECTIONS Underline the correct possessive noun in each sentence below.

4. The two (boys' / boy's) costumes were ruined by the downpour.
5. Halloween at the (Halls' / Halls's) house is the best night of the year.
6. Today, (April's and Melanie's / April and Melanie's) game might be shared on the Internet.

Students write routinely for a range of tasks, purposes, and audiences. Students practice various conventions of standard English.

Name ______________________________

Context Clues

DIRECTIONS Use the context clues in the sentences to determine the meaning of the underlined words. Write the meaning of the underlined word on the lines.

1. The team will pick up the cooler and douse their coach with ice water if they win the championship.

   ____

2. If you work hard and get many customers, your business is likely to prosper.

   ____

3. The factory workers return to work feeling rested after their two-week furlough every August.

   ____

4. When her husband finally returned from overseas, Ruth was so elated she cried.

   ____

5. Saving the lives of soldiers while under enemy attack earned the female soldier an award for valor in combat.

   ____

6. The jury decided to acquit the defendant, so he left the courthouse a free man.

   ____

7. That I sneezed at the same moment that he sneezed was a coincidence that led to a long friendship.

   ____

8. As the holidays approach, postal workers must handle the deluge of holiday mail and packages that arrive daily in tons.

   ____

9. When the maestro picked up his baton, the entire orchestra looked up and awaited his direction.

   ____

10. The campers felt safe in their haven under a rock formation while the storm raged through the park.

   ____

Students apply grade-level word analysis skills.

Name ______________________________

Benchmark Vocabulary

DIRECTIONS Write a sentence using each word.

omen   rites   processions   prostrations

Write in Response to Reading

Reread pages 50–53 of *The Egypt Game*. Melanie worked hard to help April get accepted at Wilson, including stealing her eyelashes. Did she need to do so much, or would April have been accepted anyway? Begin by clearly stating your opinion about Melanie's actions. Then list two or three reasons in support of your argument, citing evidence from the text. Write your answer below, on a separate sheet of paper, or in a new document.

Students demonstrate contextual understanding of Benchmark Vocabulary. Students read text closely and use text evidence in their written answers.

Name ______________________________

Benchmark Vocabulary

DIRECTIONS Write a sentence using each word.

dutifully disobedient summoned conscience

____

____

____

____

____

____

Write in Response to Reading

Reread pages 80–88 of *The Egypt Game*. Analyze cause and effect by examining how the plan to return to Egypt developed. Begin by clearly establishing the cause of the scheme. Use evidence from the text to analyze the effects from this cause. Explain how the characters feel and act in response to the cause. Write your answer below, on a separate sheet of paper, or in a new document.

____

____

____

____

____

____

____

____

____

____

Students demonstrate contextual understanding of Benchmark Vocabulary. Students read text closely and use text evidence in their written answers.

Name ____________________

At Work on the Great Pyramid

As I pick up the clay cups, I look across the sand and spot my father chipping away at an enormous slab of limestone with his chisel. Sweat drips onto his sandals. Soon he and other masons will begin smoothing the block into the exact size the scribes require. The scribes are the bosses here at the Great Pyramid, and they will make sure the stone has the precise dimensions and perfect right angles before the laborers begin hauling it up the ramp.

My father has been working on this project every year during the flood season for fourteen years. He says the work was going on for years before he started. Father is proud of his work and prefers it to other kinds of labor for the pharaoh. After all, he is making preparations for the afterlife that each of us can have, if only we are buried correctly. And our glorious King Khufu (KOO foo) will be buried here, protected forever in this magnificent pyramid. Some say there are already two million stone blocks in the pyramid.

Although the sun is high and hot, and I have been working since it rose, I hurry back to the area where the cooks, toolmakers, and other laborers work. I hope to catch sight of my brother, but I realize that is foolish of me. With thousands of workers here, he is nowhere to be seen. Seven years ago, he started out like me, helping to get water and baskets of bread, onions, and garlic to the workers three times a day. Now he helps pull the stone slabs from boats near the river to this great building site. The blocks weigh a few tons, and many men work together to haul them on runners.

After I return the basket of cups, a scribe directs me to see one of the cooks. As I learn from the cooks, tomorrow all the workers will enjoy a feast of fish, vegetables, and maybe even figs. I am glad that I will help prepare it. It is our ninth straight day of work, and it won't end till the sun sets, but tomorrow we will rest. If it is a good day, my father will also take home some barley seed for the new planting.

Students read a text closely to determine what the text says.

Name ____________________

Sleuth Work

Gather Evidence Circle the words that refer to moving and preparing the stone blocks in the Great Pyramid.

Gather Evidence: Extend Your Ideas What clues does the narrator provide that suggest how people built the pyramids without the aid of heavy machinery?

Ask Questions Draw a box around the narrator's sentences related to the burial process.

Ask Questions: Extend Your Ideas Write three questions you want to research about what it meant to be "buried correctly" in ancient Egypt. What sources might you use?

Make Your Case In the last two paragraphs of the article, put brackets around sentences where the narrator describes what life is like working on the Great Pyramid.

Make Your Case: Extend Your Ideas Briefly explain whether you think this life is as appealing as the narrator suggests. Cite evidence from the text to support your opinion.

Students read a text closely to determine what the text says.

Name ____________________

Writing

Narrative Writing: Write a Mystery Revise your plot sequence from Lesson 2 to note key details (clues) you will add and to show when these will be introduced in the story. Start by identifying the crucial "giveaway" clue that solves the mystery, and then work backward from that point. Make sure to consider the setting for each scene. If you come up with better ideas or discover that your initial ideas do not work, you can change your plot sequence as needed. When you have finished plotting your clues, draft one or two more pages of the mystery using a separate sheet of paper or a new document.

Conventions

Singular, Plural, and Collective Nouns

DIRECTIONS Circle the correct noun or verb that completes each sentence.

1. The neighborhood (was / were) divided about the Professor's guilt.
2. Clues to help solve a crime might be found behind curtains or under (couches / couchs).
3. The detective was determined to catch the (thiefs / thieves) who committed the crime.
4. When three (octopi / octopuses) went missing from the local aquarium, the police chief was called in to investigate the unusual crime.
5. The jury (is / are) unanimous in finding the defendant guilty.
6. (Mysterys / Mysteries) are still one of the most popular kinds of (stories / story) written today.

Students write routinely for a range of tasks, purposes, and audiences. Students practice various conventions of standard English.

Name ______________________

Benchmark Vocabulary

DIRECTIONS Write a sentence using each word.

unwieldy fiendish

Write in Response to Reading

Reread pages 106–110 of *The Egypt Game*. Do you think Elizabeth should have invited Toby and Ken to join the game? Write a paragraph expressing your opinion on this topic. Be sure to support your opinion with examples and evidence from the text and the inferences you have made about Toby and Ken. Write your answer below, on a separate sheet of paper, or in a new document.

Students demonstrate contextual understanding of Benchmark Vocabulary. Students read text closely and use text evidence in their written answers.

Name ______________________

Using Dialogue to Advance the Plot

DIRECTIONS Using evidence from the text, answer the following questions about the last paragraph on page 108 and pages 110–111 from *The Egypt Game.*

1. What effect does Elizabeth's dialogue at the top of page 110 have on what some of the other characters do?

____

____

____

____

2. On pages 110–111, how do Ken's dialogue and Toby's actions slow down the plot?

____

____

____

____

____

3. How does the dialogue on page 112 between April and Melanie show how they feel about the game moving forward?

____

____

____

____

Students analyze and respond to literary and informational text.

Name ________________________________

Narrative Writing: Balance Narration and Dialogue Draft one to two new pages to continue your story before beginning to revise your draft. As you revise, remember to balance the use of narration and dialogue to develop the plot, set a specific pace, and engage readers while allowing them to get to know the characters and remain intrigued by the plot events. Try changing some dialogue to narration or vice versa and comparing the new treatment to the one you originally used. Make sure to include all the clues readers will need to solve the mystery. Use a separate sheet of paper or start a new document.

Use Subject and Object Personal Pronouns

DIRECTIONS Complete each sentence with the correct pronoun or pronouns.

1. ____________ (I / Me) invited ____________ (they / them) to my house.
2. Mike asked ____________ (we / us) to give ____________ (he / him) our phone numbers.
3. Amy and ____________ (she / her) will bring enough snacks for everyone.
4. ____________ (We / Us) surprised everyone because ____________ (they / them) thought the party was cancelled.
5. You can rely on Peter and ____________ (I / me) to clean up afterward.
6. Did anyone tell you that Sophie and ____________ (I / me) are coming?

Students write routinely for a range of tasks, purposes, and audiences. Students practice various conventions of standard English.

Name ______________________________

Benchmark Vocabulary

DIRECTIONS Write a sentence using each word.

casualties   deciphered   rendezvous

Write in Response to Reading

Reread pages 134–138 of *The Egypt Game*. Write an explanatory paragraph that explains the steps Toby and Ken took as they participated in their first ceremony, the Ceremony for the Dead. As you explain how the boys took part, note specific words and phrases the author uses to create the tone of this scene. Also, be sure to include details and examples from the text as you write your paragraph. Write your answer below, on a separate sheet of paper, or in a new document.

Students demonstrate contextual understanding of Benchmark Vocabulary. Students read text closely and use text evidence in their written answers.

Name ____________________

Narrative Writing: Analyze Word Choice to Create Suspense Reread the draft of your mystery from beginning to end to review your word choices and the level of detail and suspense throughout. As you read, mark places where you want to

- add relevant descriptive (sensory) details or more specific details,
- use more precise words and phrases, and
- use words and phrases that can add suspense to experiences and events.

Then revise your draft to make these changes. Use a separate sheet of paper or start a new document.

Possessive and Indefinite Pronouns

DIRECTIONS Find the pronoun(s) in each sentence. Circle any possessive pronouns and underline the indefinite pronouns.

1. The prize is hers, although many think that Jason wrote a better essay.
2. Anyone can enter the contest if there is no fee.
3. I'll read yours if you read mine and make sure nothing is spelled incorrectly.
4. Something told Jenna that these essays would be better than most.
5. Everyone submitted an essay, but the judges don't know whose is whose.

Students write routinely for a range of tasks, purposes, and audiences. Students practice various conventions of standard English.

Name ______________________________

Benchmark Vocabulary

DIRECTIONS Write a sentence using each word.

pilgrimage regal presided

Write in Response to Reading

Reread pages 145–147 of *The Egypt Game*. Think about April's and Toby's actions, thoughts, feelings, and dialogue. Then, write an informative paragraph comparing and contrasting the two characters. As you explain their differences and similarities, cite text evidence that supports your inferences. Write your answer below, on a separate sheet of paper, or in a new document.

Students demonstrate contextual understanding of Benchmark Vocabulary. Students read text closely and use text evidence in their written answers.

Name ______________________________

Writing

Narrative Writing: Add Transitions to Convey Sequence and Shifts in Time and Setting Read your story and try to imagine that you are reading it for the first time. As you read, mark places where transitions may be needed to show or clarify

- the order of events,
- a shift to a different time or time period, including flashbacks, or
- a change to a different location.

If you are having trouble clarifying the sequence of events within a scene, sketch a time line or use a story sequence graphic organizer to help you. Then revise your draft to add necessary transition words, phrases, or clauses. Use a separate sheet of paper or start a new document.

Conventions

Reflexive Pronouns

DIRECTIONS Write a reflexive pronoun to complete each sentence below. Underline the subject that the reflexive pronoun refers to.

1. Vincent was proud of ____________ for making the team.
2. I can imagine ____________ forgetting to bring in my permission slip.
3. Can you find the way there ____________?
4. The puppies found a way to open the gate ____________.
5. We think of ____________ as helpful people.
6. The problem revealed ____________ after we compared notes.

Students write routinely for a range of tasks, purposes, and audiences. Students practice various conventions of standard English.

Name ____________________

Greek and Latin Roots *aero, aqua, bio, circum, dict*

Root Bank
aero, air
aqua, water
bio, life, living
circum, around, round about
dict, say, speak, proclaim

Meaning Bank
under the ocean
watchful and cautious
a liquid under pressure in a container released as a fine spray
a writer who tells someone's life story
saying something will happen before it does

DIRECTIONS On the first line, write the root from the Root Bank that appears in the word listed. On the second line, write the meaning from the Meaning Bank that matches this word.

1. prediction ____________

____

2. subaquatic ____________

____

3. aerosol ____________

____

4. circumspect ____________

____

5. biographer ____________

____

DIRECTIONS Use the words from 1–5 above to fill in the sentences below.

6. You can buy deodorant as a solid, roll-on, or ____________.
7. Doris Kearns Goodwin is a famous ____________ of Abraham Lincoln.
8. My mother's ____________ that I would win the race came true!
9. Scuba equipment allows humans to explore the ____________ world.
10. You need to be ____________ about giving out information online.

Students apply grade-level word analysis skills.

Name ______________________________

Benchmark Vocabulary

DIRECTIONS Write a sentence using each word.

steadfastly   commotion   alibi

Write in Response to Reading

On page 170 of *The Egypt Game* Toby says, "I did not. I didn't lie once. I just gave the wrong impression." Do you agree or disagree with him? Write a paragraph expressing your opinion on this topic. As you explain your thoughts, cite text evidence that supports your opinion. Write your answer below, on a separate sheet of paper, or in a new document.

Students demonstrate contextual understanding of Benchmark Vocabulary. Students read text closely and use text evidence in their written answers.

Name ______________________________

Summarize to Determine Theme

DIRECTIONS Use evidence from the text to answer the following questions about *The Egypt Game.*

1. How did April and Marshall feel once they got to Egypt? Summarize what happened when April and Marshall try to leave Egypt.

____

____

____

____

____

____

____

____

2. What is one theme you can think of that is a result of the events you just summarized and their aftermath? Provide a rationale for your answer.

____

____

____

____

____

____

Students analyze and respond to literary and informational text.

Name ______________________________

Writing

Narrative Writing: Write an Effective Conclusion Complete your mystery by writing an effective conclusion. Remember that the conclusion should follow logically from previous events—in particular, the discovery made during the climax—and from the development of characters and experiences they have. Make sure your conclusion helps readers understand how clues helped the characters solve the mystery. Your conclusion should also show how the characters have been affected by, and how they have changed because of, the events in the plot. This will help you convey any message or theme you want to share with readers. Use a separate sheet of paper or start a new document.

Conventions

Relative Pronouns

DIRECTIONS Complete each sentence with the correct relative pronoun: *who, whom, that, which,* or *whose*.

1. We went to see the movie ______________ opened last weekend.
2. The actor ______________ played the leading role was very convincing.
3. Teresa picked the movie, ______________ was my first choice, too.
4. To arrange a carpool, we discussed ______________ would drive ______________.
5. Daniel, ______________ mother has a minivan, offered to drive four people.
6. I would recommend the movie to an older brother ______________ likes science fiction.

Students write routinely for a range of tasks, purposes, and audiences. Students practice various conventions of standard English.

Name ______________________

Benchmark Vocabulary

DIRECTIONS Write a sentence using each word.

consensus speculated

Write in Response to Reading

The Egypt Game was more than just a game to the children. Given what you have learned about each character, what do you think the game meant to each of them? Write an informative paragraph that presents your ideas. Support your ideas with details from the text and the inferences you have made about the Egyptians based on the text. Write your answer below, on a separate sheet of paper, or in a new document.

Students demonstrate contextual understanding of Benchmark Vocabulary. Students read text closely and use text evidence in their written answers.

Name ______________________________

Writing

Narrative Writing: Draw Evidence to Support Analysis Write an analysis consisting of several paragraphs that explain how the author of *The Egypt Game* uses vivid descriptions and an effective plot sequence to engage readers and create suspense. Make sure to use the text evidence that you identified to support your analysis and explain how the author's use of the elements helped her craft an engaging and suspenseful mystery. Try to include brief quotes from the text that illustrate each point you are making, and include page numbers for reference. Use a separate sheet of paper or start a new document.

Conventions

Ensure Proper Case for Pronouns

DIRECTIONS Write the correct pronoun and identify its function in the sentence. Write *S* if the pronoun is the subject of the sentence, *O* if it is the object, and *P* if it is possessive.

1. I asked __________ (they / them / their) to take a step back. __________
2. __________ (We / Us / Our) had a fire drill at school today. __________
3. Tell the principal when it is __________ (you / your / yours) turn to go. __________
4. During the assembly, __________ (she / her / hers) will make an announcement. __________
5. The teacher asked Jonas and __________ (I / me / my) to prepare a speech. __________
6. Does Anita know which bus is __________ (us / our / ours)? __________

Students write routinely for a range of tasks, purposes, and audiences. Students practice various conventions of standard English.

Name ______________________________

Benchmark Vocabulary

DIRECTIONS Write a sentence using each word.

assassins flattery influence

____

____

____

____

____

____

Write in Response to Reading

Reread the second paragraph on page 10 of *You Wouldn't Want to Be Cleopatra!* where the author presents the idea that Cleopatra faces a tough job in making Egypt a great empire again. Identify and list the details and examples the author uses to develop this idea throughout the text. Write your response below, on a separate sheet of paper, or in a new document.

____

____

____

____

____

____

____

____

____

____

Students demonstrate contextual understanding of Benchmark Vocabulary. Students read text closely and use text evidence in their written answers.

Name ____________________

Key Individual

DIRECTIONS Using textual evidence, answer the following questions about pages 5–17 from *You Wouldn't Want to Be Cleopatra!*

1. What details and examples does the author provide on pages 13–17 to support the idea that Cleopatra did not live the life of a typical ancient Egyptian woman?

____

____

____

2. On page 12, we learn that Egyptian women had more freedoms than women in other parts of the ancient world. What details and examples does the author provide to develop the idea that Cleopatra experienced freedoms as well as limitations?

____

____

____

3. What details and examples does the author provide to illustrate the idea that Cleopatra was an intelligent ruler?

____

____

____

4. What details and examples does the author provide that indicate that Cleopatra relied on the support of men, but that she also felt that they could not be trusted?

____

____

____

Students analyze and respond to literary and informational text.

Name Lara Kling

Writing

Narrative Writing: Introduce and Develop a Character Use your prewriting notes to help begin writing a short story about an Egyptian king or queen who faces a problem—either humorous or serious. In your exposition, introduce the main character and then develop him or her using examples and anecdotes to set the stage for the conflict. Make sure to briefly establish the narrator and setting along with your main character and his or her problem. Use a separate sheet of paper or start a new document to begin writing your short story.

Conventions

Pronoun-Antecedent Agreement

DIRECTIONS Circle the pronoun and its antecedent in each sentence below. If the pronoun and antecedent do not agree, write the correct pronoun on the line to fix the problem.

1. The players had to protect their goal. ________
2. The visiting team accidentally scored a goal against ourselves. itself
3. The players have his own lockers. their
4. Anna and I forgot her uniforms and couldn't play in the game. our
5. The coach praised the players for its positive attitude. their
6. The game ball must be returned to their proper place. it's

Students write routinely for a range of tasks, purposes, and audiences. Students practice various conventions of standard English.

Name ____________________

Benchmark Vocabulary

DIRECTIONS Write a sentence using each word.

utterly publicity fortress

Write in Response to Reading

Imagine you are a reporter assigned to write about Cleopatra's ability to impress people. Write a short article titled "How to Win Friends and Influence People—Cleopatra Style." Relate several examples from pages 20–23 of her sensational parties and parades. Explain how and why they affected guests or observers. Write your answer below, on a separate sheet of paper, or in a new document.

Students demonstrate contextual understanding of Benchmark Vocabulary. Students read text closely and use text evidence in their written answers.

Name ____________________

Writing

Narrative Writing: Use Dialogue and Description to Develop Plot and Characters Use your plot outline and other planning notes or sketches to help you finish writing your story about an ancient Egyptian king or queen who is facing a problem. Keep in mind that dialogue and description should further develop characters' personalities while also conveying the plot events or action in the story. Remember the following techniques:

- Use dialogue to show how the characters cause, participate in, feel about, and react to events. Make sure to punctuate and capitalize the spoken words correctly.
- Make dialogue sound the way the characters would naturally talk in that situation.
- Describe relevant details about characters and plot events to help readers visualize what is happening and experience events along with the characters.

Use a separate sheet of paper or start a new document.

Conventions

Agreement with Indefinite Pronouns

DIRECTIONS Circle the indefinite pronoun in each sentence and write the correct form of the verb to complete the sentence.

1. Everybody ______________ (is / are) waiting for news about the storm.
2. The news broadcast said that anyone who ______________ (need / needs) assistance can call the emergency hotline.
3. There are few who ______________ (want / wants) to evacuate.
4. We have two emergency shelters in our neighborhood, and neither ______________ (is / are) very far from our house.
5. I think that none of the homes in this area ______________ (is / are) in danger.

Students write routinely for a range of tasks, purposes, and audiences. Students practice various conventions of standard English.

Name ______________________

Benchmark Vocabulary

DIRECTIONS Write a sentence using each word.

influence speculated

Write in Response to Reading

Reread the first full paragraph, beginning "Opposite the altar . . ." on page 54 of *The Egypt Game.* Reread the second paragraph and the section RELIGION on page 22 of *You Wouldn't Want to Be Cleopatra!* How are the uses and meanings of the Egyptian goddess Isis in the two texts alike and different? Include in your comparison whether features play a role in each of the texts.

Students demonstrate contextual understanding of Benchmark Vocabulary. Students read text closely and use text evidence in their written answers.

Name ____________________

Writing

Narrative Writing: Use Word Choice to Convey Humor Use the ideas you've gathered to help you write a humorous fictional anecdote about individuals or characters from *The Egypt Game* or *You Wouldn't Want to Be Cleopatra!* After choosing the focus of your anecdote, determine what event the anecdote will describe. Keep your anecdote to no more than one page and make sure to set a quick pace and include humorous words, phrases, expressions, and descriptions to help you convey the incident in an amusing way. Use a thesaurus to help you find funny or precise words that call a certain image to mind and engage your reader.

Conventions

Use Action Verbs

DIRECTIONS Underline the action verb in each sentence below. Then write *past, present,* or *future* to identify the tense of the verb.

1. She climbed up the ladder to the treehouse. ____________
2. After school, Brian will search his locker for his house keys. ____________
3. I always groan at my dad's bad jokes. ____________
4. Many people on an airplane will sleep during a long flight. ____________
5. The puppy chases our neighbor's pet cat. ____________
6. For five nights in a row I dreamed about the test. ____________

Students write routinely for a range of tasks, purposes, and audiences. Students practice various conventions of standard English.

Name ____ **Word Analysis**

Inferred Word Meanings

DIRECTIONS Read the paragraph. Write the meanings of the underlined words and the context clues that help you determine the meaning.

Dr. Allen was a skilled neurosurgeon who saved a patient's life. When she discovered that her patient was a veteran whose heroic accomplishments were never commended, she contacted the local newspaper about how the soldier should be venerated as a hero. However, she was chagrined to find that the journalists preferred worthless stories about psychic pets over a story about a gallant soldier.

1. accomplishments **1.** ________________________________

2. commended **2.** ________________________________

3. venerated **3.** ________________________________

4. chagrined **4.** ________________________________

5. gallant **5.** ________________________________

DIRECTIONS Write the parts of speech for the underlined words.

6. That song about knapsacks on one's back may be comparatively old-fashioned, but the lyrics are still applicable. ________________________

7. Rita's exquisite tapestry was unanimously selected to hang in the community arts museum. ________________________

8. Jake was sullen, but his testimony was consistently dependable.

____

DIRECTIONS: Match the words from above with a definition. Think about the context clues in the sentences and parts of speech.

9. sullen ______ **a.** handwoven textile

10. lyrics ______ **b.** having a bad temper

11. exquisite ______ **c.** words of a song

12. tapestry ______ **d.** always behaving in the same way

13. consistently ______ **e.** very fine

Students apply grade-level word analysis skills.

Name ______________________

Benchmark Vocabulary

DIRECTIONS Write a sentence using each word.

allies lavish concealed

____

____

____

____

Write in Response to Reading

Choose an incident or event from the poem "Cleopatra." Gather more information about the incident or event about Cleopatra from your reading and write a paragraph or poem stanza(s) as if Cleopatra were telling her own story about the event.

____

____

____

____

____

____

Students demonstrate contextual understanding of Benchmark Vocabulary. Students read text closely and use text evidence in their written answers.

Name ______________________________

Analyze Point of View

DIRECTIONS Using evidence from the text, answer the following questions about pages 18–19 from "Cleopatra."

1. What word in the first stanza gives the narrator's point of view about Cleopatra's looks?

   ____

2. Reread the third stanza. The narrator uses the words *clever, daring, fell under her spell,* and *threw lavish banquets.* How can you determine if this information is reliable?

   ____

   ____

   ____

3. A third-person narrator can present facts and serious situations without emotion. How is this technique supported by the narrator's words in the sixth stanza?

   ____

   ____

   ____

   ____

Students analyze and respond to literary and informational text.

Name ______________________________

Writing

Narrative Writing: Research a Related Topic Begin researching print and digital sources to find information about Cleopatra, her palace, and life in ancient Egypt to help you write a mystery set in Cleopatra's palace. Use a separate sheet of paper or start a new document to record your research findings. Make sure to include the following information:

- the research questions you identified,
- paraphrased answers to your questions,
- any other relevant, useful information that you find, and
- bibliographic information for each source you use: the author, the title of the source, and page number(s) or Web page address. This will help you return to the source for additional details later, if needed.

Conventions

Linking Verbs

DIRECTIONS Underline the linking verb in each sentence. Then draw a box around the subject of the sentence and circle the information that is provided about the subject.

1. Troy is excited about the field trip to a science museum.
2. Leah said the museum seems crowded for a weekday.
3. The museum tour guide was happy to answer our questions.
4. The museum's courtyard looks perfect for a picnic.
5. After looking at the food science exhibit, we all felt hungry.

Students write routinely for a range of tasks, purposes, and audiences. Students practice various conventions of standard English.

Name ______________________________

Benchmark Vocabulary

DIRECTIONS Write a sentence using each word.

flattery concealed

____

____

____

____

____

____

Write in Response to Reading

Explain how the section "Spooked!" on page 26 of *You Wouldn't Want to Be Cleopatra!* clarifies, explains, and/or contradicts the information about the battle and Cleopatra's response contained in lines 13–16 of "Cleopatra." Be sure to include evidence that supports your explanation.

____

____

____

____

____

____

Students demonstrate contextual understanding of Benchmark Vocabulary. Students read text closely and use text evidence in their written answers.

Name ____________________

Sleuth Work

It's All Greek to Us!

If you think the glory that was Greece died out long ago, think again. Those Greeks just won't leave us alone. Or maybe it's the other way around! It is common knowledge that ancient Greece was one of the cultures that had a significant influence on our literature, architecture, and democracy. But did you know that names from Greek mythology and culture are embedded in our modern life in many different areas, from sports to spacecraft to specific companies and brands?

Given the power of many ancient Greek gods and warriors, it's not surprising that we see their names in both professional and amateur sports teams. According to Greek legend, titans created the entire universe and all the lesser gods. So it makes sense that Tennessee football owners might name their professional team the Tennessee Titans. (By the way, the New York Jets used to be the New York Titans before they updated their name by a couple of millennia.) Why does Michigan State University call its team the Spartans? The Spartans came from Sparta, the Greek city-state that made an art of war and turned out the kind of fighters who beat the big odds.

Along with sporting enthusiasts, aeronautical engineers and National Aeronautics and Space Administration (NASA) scientists have found inspiration for names in Greek mythology. For example, the Apollo space mission was named after the god of the sun, who drove his chariot across the sky. The Gemini program was named after a pair of mythological twins. And then there are the Poseidon and Trident missiles, named after the Greek god of the sea and his three-pronged spear. The military folks who gave the name Hercules to a series of large transport aircraft likely had the legendary Greek strongman in mind.

You might be familiar with an online store named after the mighty Amazon River. The Spanish explorers who named that river probably had heard of a group of powerful women warriors from Greek mythology called Amazons. You may have also heard of a moving company named after Atlas, the god who carried the world on his back.

Do a little investigating. You may be surprised to discover many products and businesses named for figures in Greek mythology. Figures such as Ajax, Orion, Oracle, Pandora, and Midas have new meanings for us today. Greeks are everywhere!

Students read text closely to determine what the text says.

Name ____________________

Gather Evidence Circle one Greek name and underline information about its use in Greek history. Write the name and its use below.

____

____

Gather Evidence: Extend Your Ideas Briefly evaluate why the name and its meaning work effectively for its current use in today's world.

____

____

Ask Questions Reread the last paragraph of the article. Write one question you have about names for products and businesses. Include at least one detail from the text.

____

____

Ask Questions: Extend Your Ideas List two examples of reliable resources you could use to find the answer and explain how you might use each.

____

____

Make Your Case Bracket information that provides evidence of how widespread Greek names are in today's world. Then write a sentence summarizing this information.

____

____

Make Your Case: Extend Your Ideas What is the importance of recognizing that Greek culture has an impact on life today? Discuss your viewpoint with a partner.

____

____

Students read text closely to determine what the text says.

Name ______________________________

Writing

Narrative Writing: Plan and Prewrite Using the Story Sequence A graphic organizer and your research notes from Lesson 12, plan and prewrite a mystery that takes place in Cleopatra's palace. Your plan should include ideas and details for the beginning, middle, and end of your story. Make sure your plan includes a complete plot that is organized around a main problem or conflict. Use a separate sheet of paper or start a new document to identify and briefly describe each of the following elements of your story:

- The setting
- The main character, narrator, and additional important characters
- The problem/conflict and its solution
- The plot including main events, clues, climax, and description of the resolution or conclusion of the story

Conventions

Linking Verb or Helping Verb

DIRECTIONS Circle the linking verbs and underline the helping verbs in the sentences below.

1. Our class is learning about Viking history.
2. Storytelling was an important part of Viking culture.
3. I have memorized many details of the story we read about Odin, the Viking god.
4. The Vikings did not write down their stories, but they were skilled at retelling long sagas.
5. Thor seemed more powerful than Odin, even though Odin was the father of the gods and had used magic to do amazing things.

Students write routinely for a range of tasks, purposes, and audiences. Students practice various conventions of standard English.

Name ______________________________

Benchmark Vocabulary

DIRECTIONS Write a sentence using each word.

fragment inscribed propaganda

Write in Response to Reading

Reread paragraph 5 on page 11, beginning "Despite their exhaustive search . . ." Describe how Calliope responds to the discovery of the second message, instead of the piece of stone she and Julian had hoped to find. What effect do you think this new message will have on Calliope? Support your ideas with details from the text and the inferences you have made about Calliope based on the text.

Students demonstrate contextual understanding of Benchmark Vocabulary. Students read text closely and use text evidence in their written answers.

Name ______________________________

Cause and Effect

DIRECTIONS Using evidence from the text, answer the following questions about pages 4–11 from *Calliope's History Mystery*.

1. What effect does the family's arrival in Cairo on page 5 have on Calliope?

2. On page 7, Calliope's father says, "If the two of you find the fragment . . . you'll make history!" How does his promise affect the characters and the plot?

3. What happens on page 8 when Calliope enters the large room with the statues? What effect, if any, does this event have on her character and on the plot?

4. Reread Calliope's mother's explanation on page 10. Based on her explanation, what was one likely cause of Ramesses II's powerful reign?

Students analyze and respond to literary and informational text.

Name ____

Writing

Narrative Writing: Draft a Mystery Use your completed Story Sequence A graphic organizer as well as your research notes to draft a mystery that takes place in Cleopatra's palace. Your goal for this first draft is to tell the whole story from beginning to end. Try to write continuously, without stopping to revise or edit. Your draft should include the following:

- A beginning that establishes the narrator, main characters, and setting and introduces the conflict
- A middle that includes a sequence of events following a rising action and climax, and clues and suspects that lead up to the climatic event
- An end that includes the falling action and a resolution to the problem in which the mystery is solved and the final outcome for characters is revealed

Use a separate sheet of paper or start a new document to write your draft.

Conventions

Linking Verbs and Subject Complements

DIRECTIONS Find the linking verb in each sentence below. Circle the subject and underline the subject complement.

1. In this section of the museum, all of the artifacts are Egyptian.
2. The hieroglyphic writing on this tablet looks different from the writing on that one.
3. Jeffrey said that the wood coffin seems too small to hold an adult person.
4. The archaeologists found proof that the coins in this case were real gold.
5. Deena was waiting for the museum's collection to become larger before she visited again.

Students write routinely for a range of tasks, purposes, and audiences. Students practice various conventions of standard English.

Name ______________________

Benchmark Vocabulary

DIRECTIONS Write a sentence using each word.

indicate miniature

Write in Response to Reading

Reread the dialogue between Calliope and Julian on page 13. What can you infer about their relationship? Write a paragraph that explains the inference you made and includes examples and details from the text to support it. Write your paragraph below, on a separate sheet of paper, or in a new document.

Students demonstrate contextual understanding of Benchmark Vocabulary. Students read text closely and use text evidence in their written answers.

Name ______________________________

Writing

Narrative Writing: Review and Revise a Mystery Review the first draft of your mystery that takes place in Cleopatra's palace. Review your draft for: (1) a clear and logical sequence of events; (2) a balanced amount of narration and dialogue; (3) multiple clues that are not too easy to figure out; and (4) specific words, phrases, and details that convey danger, uncertainty, and surprise. To revise your draft, incorporate the following actions:

- Removing ideas, information, or details that are repetitive or off-topic.
- Adding ideas, words, or phrases for interest, clarity, and support.
- Replacing deleted text by substituting new words, sentences, and paragraphs.
- Rearranging sentences and paragraphs when events are not in logical order.

Use a separate sheet of paper or start a new document.

Conventions

Principal Parts of Regular Verbs

DIRECTIONS Identify the principle part, or form, of the underlined regular verb in each sentence. Write *present, present participle, past,* or *past participle*.

1. Historians do not always agree on the meaning of past events. ____________
2. I was interested in learning more about Genghis Khan and the Mongols.

   ____
3. The Mongols and the Vikings both invaded other lands. ____________
4. Amrita is watching a movie about the Mongols that is based on a true story.

   ____
5. David said that he has watched the same movie twice already.

   ____

Students write routinely for a range of tasks, purposes, and audiences. Students practice various conventions of standard English.

Name ____________________

Benchmark Vocabulary

DIRECTIONS Write a sentence using each word.

fragment   inscribed

Write in Response to Reading

Identify important details that give information about how Calliope's relationship with her brother changes in the story. Use the important details to determine a theme for the story. Write a paragraph that states the theme and summarizes the text evidence that supports it. Write your answer below, on a separate sheet of paper, or in a new document.

Students demonstrate contextual understanding of Benchmark Vocabulary. Students read text closely and use text evidence in their written answers.

Name ____

Narrative Writing: Edit and Proofread a Mystery Edit the draft of the mystery story that you revised in the previous lesson to prepare it for publication. Read each sentence of your story carefully and identify and correct any of the following mistakes:

- Capitalization errors in proper nouns
- Incorrectly punctuated dialogue
- Improper use of pronoun case or agreement
- Lack of subject-verb agreement
- Any additional spelling, capitalization, grammar, and punctuation errors, especially those pertaining to conventions that you have reviewed in this module

When you have finished editing, create a final, clean draft that includes all of your changes and corrections. Use a separate sheet of paper or start a new document.

Principal Parts of Irregular Verbs

DIRECTIONS Write the correct present, present participle, past, or past participle form of the given irregular verb to complete each sentence.

1. Her laptop ____________ when she dropped it.
   break (past)

2. The owner ____________ a sign up every time the store has a sale.
   hang (present)

3. You are ____________ that the store closes on Sundays.
   forget (present participle)

4. I was surprised to see how much he has ____________ since last year.
   grow (past participle)

5. We cheered when the baseball player ____________ the ball.
   catch (past)

6. The buses will leave as soon as the students have ____________ lunch.
   eat (past participle)

Students write routinely for a range of tasks, purposes, and audiences. Students practice various conventions of standard English.

Name ____________________

Morphemes

Morpheme Bank

anti-	-ation
geo-	-able
pre-	-ic
re-	-ist
sub-	-or
un-	-ment

DIRECTIONS Use the given base word and one or more word parts from the Morpheme Bank to create a new word that matches each definition. Write the new word on the line.

1. Not able to be pictured in the mind: _____ imagine _____
2. A person who works under a lead builder: _____ contract _____
3. Relating to the pull or attraction of the Earth: _____ magnet _____
4. A person who wants to change how we see history: _____ vision _____
5. A condition settled beforehand: _____ establish _____
6. Able to be soaked in again and again: _____ absorb _____
7. Under the size of the smallest unit of matter: _____ atom _____

DIRECTIONS Identify the morphemes in each word. On the line, show the morphemes by writing the letters that represent each one, leaving a space between each morpheme. For example: **re settle ment.** You may need to change the spelling of a morpheme.

8. underachiever ____________________
9. dishonesty ____________________
10. ineffective ____________________
11. micromanager ____________________
12. misunderstand ____________________

Students apply grade-level word analysis skills.

Name ____

Benchmark Vocabulary

DIRECTIONS Write a sentence using each word.

cultivated regal

Write in Response to Reading

In *You Wouldn't Want to Be Cleopatra!* reread the section "A Tough Act to Follow!" on page 12 in the main text and the section "Religion" on page 22. In *The Egypt Game*, reread the first full paragraph on page 54. Write a paragraph to compare and contrast how the goddess Isis is presented in each text, focusing on appearance, function, and importance. Then state how this information demonstrates each author's approach to the topic of Egyptian goddesses.

Students demonstrate contextual understanding of Benchmark Vocabulary. Students read text closely and use text evidence in their written answers.

Name ______________________________

Compare and Contrast

DIRECTIONS Using evidence from the text, answer the following questions about *The Egypt Game, You Wouldn't Want to Be Cleopatra!,* "Cleopatra," and *Calliope's History Mystery.*

1. At the end of *Calliope's History Mystery,* Calliope realizes there is importance in learning about and trying to understand ancient people. How does her realization compare with how the children in *The Egypt Game* felt about Egypt?

2. Compare and contrast the more personal approach to Cleopatra in *You Wouldn't Want to Be Cleopatra!* and the more general approach in the poem, "Cleopatra."

3. Page 54 of *The Egypt Game* explains how pharaohs and queens were related to gods and goddesses. How does this information help clarify why Cleopatra dressed for dinner as described in the third stanza of "Cleopatra"?

Students analyze and respond to literary and informational text.

Name ____________________

Writing

Narrative Writing: Publish and Present a Mystery Publish the final draft of your mystery that takes place in Cleopatra's palace by typing your final draft using a word processing program or online document-sharing application. Then print out a copy of your final draft and annotate it for presentation, marking where to adjust rate, phrasing, and expression. Finally, present your mystery orally to the class.

Conventions

Principal Parts of *To Be*

DIRECTIONS Write a sentence that uses the named form of the verb *to be*. Use a different subject for each sentence using the past form of the verb and each sentence using the past participle form.

1. (present) ____________________

2. (present participle) ____________________

3. (past) ____________________

4. (past participle) ____________________

5. (past) ____________________

6. (past participle) ____________________

Students write routinely for a range of tasks, purposes, and audiences. Students practice various conventions of standard English.

Name ________________________________

Benchmark Vocabulary

DIRECTIONS Write a sentence using each word.

deciphered flattery lavish

Write in Response to Reading

On page 16 of *Calliope's History Mystery,* the narrator states about Calliope: "She remembered how she'd dismissed ancient dead people as unimportant and realized she had, in a way, met many of them today." Write a short paragraph explaining what Calliope means and what she is implying about the past. Write a second paragraph relating your interpretation of this quote to the other three texts, explaining how they each involved a similar kind of meeting, with important effects. Write your paragraphs below or on a separate sheet of paper.

Students demonstrate contextual understanding of Benchmark Vocabulary. Students read text closely and use text evidence in their written answers.

Name ________________________________

Narrative Writing: Conduct Research to Explore Theme Conduct research on a real-life archaeologist or paleontologist in order to identify a theme relating to treasuring history, and use your findings to write a short fictional narrative about a character who uncovers a clue about an ancient culture.

- Remember to generate questions that focus your search and help you identify subject key words.
- Analyze your findings to identify a theme relating to the idea of treasuring history. You may want to clarify your theme idea by stating it in a sentence.
- Refer to findings as you jot down ideas for a main character, a setting, and a plot that revolves around the discovery of a clue about an ancient culture.
- Write your narrative. Use a separate sheet of paper or start a new document.

Spell Correctly

DIRECTIONS Read each sentence and underline the word that is spelled incorrectly. Write the correct spelling of the word on the line.

1. She accidentally let go of the balloons and they floated up to the sealing.

____

2. Rainwater carried by gutters on the barn roof flows into the drinking troff.

____

3. Let's use a different microfone so this recording will have less background noise.

____

4. I'll have to check with my parents to see if I'll be aloud to attend the concert next week.

____

Students write routinely for a range of tasks, purposes, and audiences. Students practice various conventions of standard English.

Name ______________________________

Benchmark Vocabulary

DIRECTIONS Write a sentence using each word.

conducted advanced distinct

____

____

____

____

____

____

Write in Response to Reading

Reread the final paragraph on page 6. Use details, examples, or anecdotes from the chapter to write an opinion paragraph explaining whether you agree or disagree with the author's central idea that the Maya were an "advanced people." Write your answer below, on a separate sheet of paper, or in a new document.

____

____

____

____

____

____

____

____

____

____

Students demonstrate contextual understanding of Benchmark Vocabulary. Students read text closely and use text evidence in their written answers.

Name ______________________________

Informative/Explanatory Writing: Analyze Features and Purpose of an Encyclopedia Article After you have read your article about the Maya, write a paragraph analyzing what the article explains, how it is organized and formatted, and the kind of language and vocabulary the writer uses. Develop your paragraph with relevant details, examples, and domain-specific vocabulary while maintaining a formal style. Use a separate sheet of paper or start a new document.

Simple Verb Tenses for Regular and Irregular Verbs

DIRECTIONS Compete each sentence by writing the correct verb form on the line.

1. After the game, the two Maya teams wearily ____________ (leaved / left) the ball field.
2. When the Maya built their cities, the ancient people first ____________ (cleared / clear) the jungle.
3. The Maya calendar ____________ (astonished / astonish) scientists with its accuracy when it was first discovered.
4. Today, archaeologists ____________ (studied / study) ruins uncovered in the jungles.
5. If archaeologists ____________ (am / are / is) careless with artifacts, the artifacts can be ruined.
6. Someday I ____________ (traveled / will travel) around the world to see these ancient places.

Students write routinely for a range of tasks, purposes, and audiences. Students practice various conventions of standard English.

Name ______________________________

Word Analysis

Latin Roots *form, jud, aud, cred*

WORD BANK

incredulous	prejudicial	judgment	discredit
credence	informality	audible	creditor
incredible	formative	judicial	transform
nonconformist	audiovisual	audience	adjudicate

DIRECTIONS Write a word from the list that fits the meaning of each definition.

1. shapes the growth of something **1.** ______________
2. belief in something as true **2.** ______________
3. to act as a judge **3.** ______________
4. an opinion or decision **4.** ______________
5. using both sight and sound **5.** ______________

DIRECTIONS Write a word from the list to complete each sentence.

6. A ______________ decision on the criminal case is expected soon.
7. Gabe has the ______________ skill of creating origami from the tiniest slips of paper.
8. The attorney tried to ______________ the key witness by asking about his wild youth.
9. The candidate spoke in a barely ______________ voice during his speech.
10. The ______________ of the wedding was surprising in that the bride and groom were not wearing shoes!
11. The ruler wants to ______________ the country from a traditional monarchy into a modern democracy.
12. Joe's ______________ gave him an extension of two weeks to repay his debt.
13. The people in the ______________ heard the most striking piano performance.
14. Pam's ______________ attitude helped her to create original designs.
15. My friend's ______________ opinion that eggs are only eaten for breakfast is not shared by my family.
16. I was ______________ that I needed a parent's note just to eat my lunch outside.

Students apply grade-level word analysis skills.

Name ______________________________

Benchmark Vocabulary

DIRECTIONS Write a sentence using each word.

foundation orderly horizontal

Write in Response to Reading

Reread the text about the Maya view of the universe on pages 12–14. Use key details including examples, facts, or anecdotes from the chapter to write an informative/explanatory paragraph that compares and contrasts the Maya view of the world with your own. Write your answer below, on a separate sheet of paper, or in a new document.

Students demonstrate contextual understanding of Benchmark Vocabulary. Students read text closely and use text evidence in their written answers.

Name ____

Key Details

DIRECTIONS Using evidence from the text, answer the following questions about pages 12–19 from *The Ancient Maya.*

1. Reread details on page 14 about the Maya god, Chak. How do these details support the idea that the Maya gods were complex beings?

2. How do the details in the photo and caption on page 15 support information in the text about the Maya people's understanding of the universe?

3. Reread the details that describe the rules of pok-a-tok on page 19. What do you learn about the purpose of this game based on the rules?

Students analyze and respond to literary and informational text.

Name ____________________

Writing

Informative/Explanatory Writing: Choose a Topic Take notes during your topic selection process, writing the steps you took to find a suitable topic. Then write a paragraph explaining how you chose your final topic. In your paragraph, tell the topic you originally chose and your original search terms. Then explain how your search results helped you select your final topic. Write your paragraph on a separate sheet of paper or start a new document.

Conventions

Perfect Tense

DIRECTIONS Write the correct verb form on the line provided in each sentence.

1. I ____________ (have chosen / have chose) to write about the objects recovered from the Sacred Well.
2. Scientists found gold and silver jewelry that Maya priests ____________ (had thrown / had threw) into the well.
3. They also discovered carved figurines the rulers ____________ (have sacrificed / had sacrificed) to the rain god.
4. Thousands of tourists ____________ (have went / have gone) to see the Sacred Well for themselves.

DIRECTIONS Complete the chart.

Verb	Present Perfect	Past Perfect	Future Perfect
calculate	have calculated		
be			
fly			

Students write routinely for a range of tasks, purposes, and audiences. Students practice various conventions of standard English.

Name ______________________________

Benchmark Vocabulary

DIRECTIONS Write a sentence using each word.

vertical descent

____

____

____

____

Write in Response to Reading

Reread "The Sacred Book" on page 23. Then review the descriptions of pok-a-tok on pages 4–5 and pages 18–19. Use details, examples, or anecdotes from the chapters to write an explanatory paragraph that tells how the story of the Hero Twins is reflected in the game of pok-a-tok. Write your answer below, on a separate sheet of paper, or in a new document.

____

____

____

____

____

____

____

____

____

____

____

____

Students demonstrate contextual understanding of Benchmark Vocabulary. Students read text closely and use text evidence in their written answers.

Name ____

Journey Back in Time

Let's take a trip back in time more than 3,000 years ago to the west banks of the Nile River. Imagine working to build one of the many pyramids constructed in the rocks of Egypt's Valley of the Kings. Without iron tools, the laborers' work was difficult. It could take decades to build the complex structures; most included staircases, chambers, and narrow passageways.

The kings had the pyramids built as burial places for themselves and their families. The ancient Egyptians believed the soul lived on after death and that the bodies needed to be preserved to experience the afterlife. Furthermore, they believed that a person's possessions should be buried with the body. Through the years, thieves looted the pyramids hoping to steal gold and other treasures.

However, in 1922, Howard Carter discovered a tomb that raiders had overlooked. King Tut's burial chamber had remained undisturbed for thousands of years. It still contained most of the king's possessions. Besides finding the young king's mummified body, Carter discovered four rooms filled with breathtaking items. The more than 5,000 objects included Tut's gold mask and throne, jewelry, statues, and furniture. The discovery sparked widespread interest in ancient Egypt and offered important clues to the ancient Egyptians' beliefs, customs, and culture.

Now let's take another trip back in time. More than 500 years ago, a city perched in the Andes (AN deez) Mountains of Peru was home to a thriving civilization. The ascent to the city was steep, almost straight up in some places. Having heard rumors of a "lost" city, historian Hiram Bingham led an expedition to the region in 1911.

On the mountain's sides, Bingham noticed stairways skillfully cut into rock and found burial caves with skeletons and well-preserved pots. His men observed the ruins of temples and houses. Machu Picchu (MAH choo PEE choo) was divided into groups of homes with one entrance and a clever locking device. Artisans had cut the locks into granite using only primitive tools.

Machu Picchu was built in the fifteenth century as an emperor's retreat. The city was an ideal refuge protected by nature. A narrow ridge on one side connected Machu Picchu to another city, but terraces had been constructed to make attack nearly impossible. Bingham's group brought back thousands of artifacts from the city. The treasures included skeletons, ceramic pottery, stoneware, bronze, and jewelry. These relics provide a fascinating glimpse into life in the Incan Empire at the height of its power.

Students read text closely to determine what the text says.

Name ______________________________

Sleuth Work

Gather Evidence Underline text details regarding ancient Egyptian religious beliefs and architecture.

Gather Evidence: Extend Your Ideas Review the text details you underlined. What is the central idea of this part of the text? Discuss your ideas with a partner.

Ask Questions Based on the text, write two questions you have for Howard Carter or Hiram Bingham about his excavation work.

Ask Questions: Extend Your Ideas Use evidence from the text to write how Howard Carter might respond to a question about the difference between his work and the work of thieves who raid the tombs.

Make Your Case Box details regarding the customs and culture of the ancient Egyptians. Bracket details regarding the customs and culture of the ancient Inca.

Make Your Case: Extend Your Ideas How are Inca and Maya civilizations similar and different? Write your ideas below.

Students read text closely to determine what the text says.

Name ____________________

Informative/Explanatory Writing: Research a Topic List the sources you have selected to use to research your topic and provide the bibliographic information you will need to find each source again. Make sure you have researched your questions adequately so that you have a variety of at least eight to ten credible print and digital sources. Write your list on the lines below.

____

____

____

____

____

____

____

____

____

____

Verb Sequences

DIRECTIONS Circle each correct verb tense to complete the sentences.

1. In times of drought, the Maya (believed / had believed) that the rain god Chak (abandoned / had abandoned) them.
2. After the explorer (had dived / dived) into the Sacred Well, he suddenly (realized / had realized) that his air hose was not connected.
3. The priest reached the altar only to discover that he (forgot / had forgotten) his sacred knife.
4. In winter, the rulers (had predicted / predicted) abundant rainfall, but the rains (had failed / failed) to come in spring.
5. Researchers (found / had found) to their amazement that the Maya (had created / created) an extremely accurate calendar.
6. The calendar not only recorded the movements of the sun and moon but (foretold / had foretold) important events in Maya history.

Students write routinely for a range of tasks, purposes, and audiences. Students practice various conventions of standard English.

Name ______________________________

Benchmark Vocabulary

DIRECTIONS Write a sentence using each word.

professional   permanently   primary

____
____
____
____
____
____

Write in Response to Reading

Review the details in Chapter 4 of *The Ancient Maya* that describe some elements of the daily life of the four classes of Maya society: nobility, professionals, commoners, slaves. Write a summary about one class, citing evidence from the text.

____
____
____
____
____
____
____
____
____
____

Students demonstrate contextual understanding of Benchmark Vocabulary. Students read text closely and use text evidence in their written answers.

Name ______________________________

Summarize

DIRECTIONS Using evidence from the text, answer the following questions about pages 28–35 from *The Ancient Maya.*

1. Page 32 is mostly about the role of farmers in Maya society. Write a brief summary describing information about Maya farming practices.

____

____

____

____

2. The last paragraph on page 32 and most of page 34 discuss Maya slaves. Write a brief summary about the role of slaves in Maya society.

____

____

____

____

3. Provide supporting details from page 35 to support this sample summary statement about commoners in Maya society: The hard work of commoners made the Maya market a busy place where many goods were sold.

____

____

____

____

Students analyze and respond to literary and informational text.

Name ______________________________

Writing

Informative/Explanatory Writing: Take Notes Take notes on note cards using the sources you chose. Paraphrase each important piece of information on a separate card and include the author, title, and page number where you found the information. Make sure you locate necessary publishing information for each source so you can format the citation correctly in your reference list. Write your reference list below.

____

____

____

____

Conventions

Modal Auxiliary Verbs

DIRECTIONS Write the modal auxiliary verb that best completes the sentence. At the end of the sentence, write the condition that the modal auxiliary verb expresses: obligation, ability, permission, future, necessity, possibility.

1. We know for sure that he ____________ (will / might) show up Saturday night. ____________
2. She asked, "____________ (Must / Would) you like to see the Maya exhibit at the museum?" ____________
3. Many people think you ____________ (should / could) always preserve artifacts of the past. ____________
4. "____________ (May / Will) I please ask a question about that piece of pottery?" she asked. ____________
5. At the central market, the farmers ____________ (should / could) sell their crops. ____________
6. The leader ____________ (must not / may not) neglect his duty to the people. ____________

Students write routinely for a range of tasks, purposes, and audiences. Students practice various conventions of standard English.

Name ______________________________

Benchmark Vocabulary

DIRECTIONS Write a sentence using each word.

decline proposed massive imposed

Write in Response to Reading

Reread pages 41 and 43 of *The Ancient Maya*. Integrate information from the text and visuals to write an informative/explanatory paragraph that tells about the fall and survival of Maya civilization. Write your answer below, on a separate sheet of paper, or in a new document.

Students demonstrate contextual understanding of Benchmark Vocabulary. Students read text closely and use text evidence in their written answers.

Name ______________________________

Writing

Informative/Explanatory Writing: Organize Ideas Classify and organize the notes you wrote in Lesson 4 into groups according to main and supporting ideas. Next, arrange the groups of cards for each main and supporting idea into increasing levels of detail. Then, use the groups of cards to develop and write an outline for your article. Remember to use Roman numerals to list main ideas, capital letters for supporting ideas, numbers for supporting details, and lowercase letters for the most specific details. Consider how using main ideas as headings and supporting ideas as subheadings might help you format your articles. Also consider and indicate where graphics and multimedia items might be used. When you are satisfied that you have classified and organized your notes in a way that makes sense, write your outline on a separate sheet of paper or start a new document.

Conventions

Consistency in Verb Tense

DIRECTIONS Write the correct verb tense on the line provided in each sentence.

1. The Spanish brought many European diseases, and the Maya ____________ (have / had) no defense against them.
2. As scholars study Maya texts, they ____________ (are / were) amazed at the Maya's sophisticated writing system.
3. In the past, many cultures ____________ (abandon / abandoned) their cities after the local climate changed.
4. No one knew about the ancient Maya cities for centuries, because the jungle ____________ (has swallowed / had swallowed) them.

DIRECTIONS The sentences below contain inconsistent verb tenses. Correct the underlined verb to make each sentence consistent.

1. We travelled first to Tikal and then <u>visit</u> the temple at Chichén Itzá.

   ____

2. When the Spanish <u>burn</u> many Maya books, historians lost a wealth of information. ____________

Students write routinely for a range of tasks, purposes, and audiences. Students practice various conventions of standard English.

Name ______________________________

Benchmark Vocabulary

DIRECTIONS Write a sentence using each word.

advanced foundation

Write in Response to Reading

Reread the last paragraph on page 5, which concludes on page 6. Provide a summary explaining how the Maya were successful at bridging the gap between the natural and supernatural worlds for more than 2,000 years but ultimately failed as their civilization declined. Provide only important text-based details that relate to the central idea of the text. Write your answer below, on a separate sheet of paper, or in a new document.

Students demonstrate contextual understanding of Benchmark Vocabulary. Students read text closely and use text evidence in their written answers.

Name ____________________ Writing

Informative/Explanatory Writing: Develop a Topic Choose a topic that interests you and write two paragraphs to inform readers about it. State your topic in your first paragraph and develop one or two main ideas using facts, definitions, specific details, and examples. Write a second paragraph to develop one or two more main ideas about the topic. Write your paragraphs using a formal style, reporting facts objectively (without judgment), and avoiding slang, contractions, and conversational language. Write your paragraphs on a separate sheet of paper or start a new document.

Conventions

Intensive Pronouns

DIRECTIONS Decide if the underlined word is used as an intensive or reflexive pronoun. Write *intensive* or *reflexive* on the line.

1. The Maya ruler <u>himself</u> had to shed blood. ____________
2. The nobility often fought among <u>themselves</u> to gain power. ____________
3. We studied the Maya <u>ourselves</u>. ____________

DIRECTIONS Fill in the correct intensive pronoun on the lines provided.

1. The archaeologist ____________ read the Maya hieroglyphics.
2. I read about the lost cities, so I wanted to see the sites ____________.
3. She asked me, "Would you dive into a dark well ____________ and explore its depths?"

Students write routinely for a range of tasks, purposes, and audiences. Students practice various conventions of standard English.

Name ______________________________

Personification

DIRECTIONS Circle the object or idea that is being personified. Then write the human quality or action that is given to the object or idea.

1. The hungry video game ate all my quarters and never let me play.

____

2. Ms. Martin's chalk screeched a warning that our reports are due on Monday.

____

3. The ice cream in the freezer called to me. ____________

4. My heart danced the jitterbug while I waited for my turn to speak. ____________

5. My tablet pitches a fit every time I try to download the app. ____________

6. Greed stole my money. ____________

7. Silence crept into the classroom as the teacher walked in. ____________

8. The prancing maple leaf paraded across the path and stopped to rest on the forest floor. ____________

9. The bread jumped out of the toaster. ____________

10. The phone disrupted the meeting with an angry ring.

____

11. Thunder grumbled to the picnickers that it was time to go home. ____________

12. She felt as if danger were lurking in the shadows. ____________

Students apply grade-level word analysis skills.

Name ______________________________

Benchmark Vocabulary

DIRECTIONS Write a sentence using each word.

vivid durable substances

____

____

____

____

____

____

Write in Response to Reading

Reread pages 83 and 85 of "Secret to Mayan Blue Paint Found." Summarize the significance of blue paint in ancient Mayan culture. Use details, examples, and key ideas from the selection in your summary. Write your answer below, on a separate sheet of paper, or in a new document.

____

____

____

____

____

____

____

Students demonstrate contextual understanding of Benchmark Vocabulary. Students read text closely and use text evidence in their written answers.

Name ________________________________

Summarize

DIRECTIONS Using evidence from the text, answer the following questions about "Secret to Mayan Blue Paint Found."

1. Provide details that explain the relationship of Chichén Itzá to the central idea of the article as expressed in paragraph 1 on page 83.

____

____

____

2. Explain how the title of the selection supports the central idea of the text.

____

____

____

3. Provide details that support and explain the following summary statement: The Maya valued the color blue.

____

____

____

4. Which supporting details from the captions and illustrations could be used in a summary of the selection?

____

____

____

____

____

____

Students analyze and respond to literary and informational text.

Name ______________________________

Writing

Informative/Explanatory Writing: Introduce a Topic Write an introduction that introduces the topic of the two paragraphs you wrote in Lesson 6. Your introductory paragraph should clearly introduce the topic, state what the following paragraphs will cover in the order in which information will be presented, and be written in a formal style.

____

____

____

____

Conventions

Pronoun Shifts in Number

DIRECTIONS Circle the incorrect pronoun in each sentence and write the correct pronoun on the line provided.

1. I reached the hilltop alone, and we could see the entire valley below. ______
2. Anyone who arrives early can choose their seat on the bus. ______________

   ____
3. Many students wanted to use his tablet to record a few notes. ______
4. Carl and Andre said their tour was great, although he didn't sleep very much.

   ______
5. Tia and Briana expected some cloudy days, but she didn't think it would rain all the time. ______
6. Linus and I wanted to work on an archaeology site, so he went to Cahokia in Illinois. ______

Students write routinely for a range of tasks, purposes, and audiences. Students practice various conventions of standard English.

Name ______________________________

Benchmark Vocabulary

DIRECTIONS Write a sentence using each word.

distinct substances

Write in Response to Reading

Reread page 5 of *The Ancient Maya* and pages 83 and 85 of "Secret to Mayan Blue Paint Found." Then compare and integrate information from both texts to write an informative/explanatory paragraph that supports the central idea that the ancient Maya tried to "bridge the gap between the natural and supernatural worlds." Write your answer below, on a separate sheet of paper, or in a new document.

Students demonstrate contextual understanding of Benchmark Vocabulary. Students read text closely and use text evidence in their written answers.

Name ______________________________

Writing

Informative/Explanatory Writing: Use Images, Graphics, and Multimedia Elements Determine what images, graphics, or multimedia materials you want to use for the paragraphs you wrote in Lessons 6 and 7 and where each element will be placed. Then research digital and print media or use software to create your own materials. Keep in mind that you can use photos and illustrations to present details or information; use graphics to present or summarize information; and use music, sound effects, or video to bring the topic to life. List and describe the placement of your images, graphics, and multimedia materials and their sources, including a credit if necessary, on a separate sheet of paper or start a new document.

Conventions

Pronoun Shifts in Person

DIRECTIONS Change the underlined pronoun in each sentence to correct the shift in person. Write the correct pronoun on the line.

1. When we asked about Maya relics, <u>you</u> could see the professor loved the topic.

   ____

2. Every time you see a relic from the past, <u>they</u> find it strangely fascinating.

   ____

3. They wanted to know what special pigments <u>you</u> could make from scratch.

   ____

4. If I follow directions, <u>everyone</u> should be able to make blue paint. ________
5. You should always be careful when <u>they</u> are painting fragile pottery. ________

Students write routinely for a range of tasks, purposes, and audiences. Students practice various conventions of standard English.

Name ____________________

Benchmark Vocabulary

DIRECTIONS Write a sentence using each word.

remote harmony dominate proclaimed

____

____

____

____

____

____

____

____

Write in Response to Reading

Reread pages 22, 25, and 28. Use evidence from the text and the accompanying photographs, illustrations, and captions to write an informational paragraph about how archaeologists and others use their discoveries to learn about Inka culture. Write your answer below, on a separate sheet of paper, or in a new document.

____

____

____

____

____

____

____

____

____

Students demonstrate contextual understanding of Benchmark Vocabulary. Students read text closely and use text evidence in their written answers.

Name ___

Central Idea

DIRECTIONS Using evidence from the text, answer the following questions about pages 20–29 from *Machu Picchu.*

1. On page 22, the author describes the discovery of Machu Picchu in 1911 and comments that it is "a haunting place." How does this comment relate to the central idea?

2. What effect did the Spanish explorers' invasion of the Andes have on our knowledge of the Inkas?

3. Reread page 25. What evidence from the text explains how archaeologists know about these aspects of Inka culture?

4. How does the information on page 29 support the central idea of the text?

Students analyze and respond to literary and informational text.

Name ______________________________________

Writing

Informative/Explanatory Writing: Use Compare-and-Contrast Text Structure Use your planning ideas and notes to write a compare-and-contrast paragraph that tells how some aspect of Maya or Inka culture compares to your own culture. Remember to use a clear compare-and-contrast structure that is consistent throughout, include domain-specific vocabulary to make your ideas clear, use transitional words and phrases to show how ideas connect, and use a formal writing style. Write your compare-and-contrast paragraph on a separate sheet of paper or start a new document.

Conventions

Recognizing and Correcting Vague Pronouns

DIRECTIONS Circle the vague pronoun in each sentence and correct the error on the lines provided.

1. Elizabeth Mann's *Machu Picchu* describes the rise and fall of Inka civilization. It was long and exciting. ____________________

2. The expedition members told the peasant boys that they had located an Inka mountain settlement. ____________________

3. Archaeologists are learning more about the Inkas. This reveals striking differences between Inka culture and modern culture. ____________________

4. After defeating enemies in battles, Pachacuti often dishonored them.

____

Students write routinely for a range of tasks, purposes, and audiences. Students practice various conventions of standard English.

Name ___________________________________

Benchmark Vocabulary

DIRECTIONS Write a sentence using each word.

privileges menacing genius supreme

____
____
____
____
____
____
____
____

Write in Response to Reading

Reread the first paragraph on page 34 of *Machu Picchu*, and decide if you agree with this statement: "Weaving the many different peoples into a unified nation was the real work, and the true genius, of the Inkas." State your opinion and use evidence from the text to support your reasons. Write your answer below, on a separate sheet of paper, or in a new document.

____
____
____
____
____
____

Students demonstrate contextual understanding of Benchmark Vocabulary. Students read text closely and use text evidence in their written answers.

Name ____________________

Informative/Explanatory Writing: Use a Cause-and-Effect Paragraph Structure Use your planning ideas and notes to write a cause-and-effect paragraph to explain how and why your life would change if you lived in the Inka Empire. Be sure to use a cause-and-effect structure and a formal writing style, avoiding slang, contractions and conversational language. Include details about the Inka Empire that make its way of life different from yours. Use appropriate transitions to indicate cause-and-effect relationships, such as *therefore, consequently, thus,* and *as a result*. Write your paragraph on a separate sheet of paper or start a new document.

Adjectives

DIRECTIONS For each sentence, circle the adjectives and underline the nouns they modify.

1. In the Andes, Inka cities sometimes perched between mountain peaks.
2. Pachacuti rebuilt Cuzco, replacing adobe huts with a magnificent city of stone.
3. The Inkas used an ingenious method of keeping records, tying knots in *khipus*, which were fringes of colored strings.
4. A very religious people, the Inkas forced conquered tribes to worship new gods.
5. The Inkas practiced a complicated religion and kept sacred objects at Cuzco.
6. For the Inkas, melted snow from mountains was a trusted source of precious water.

Students write routinely for a range of tasks, purposes, and audiences. Students practice various conventions of standard English.

Name ______________________________

Benchmark Vocabulary

DIRECTIONS Write a sentence using each word.

vital hostile primitive trial and error

Write in Response to Reading

Reread pages 41–44 of *Machu Picchu* and select one impressive feature of the building of this community. Write a paragraph to explain what was so remarkable about the aspect you chose. Use details and examples from the text to support your answer. Write your answer below, on a separate sheet of paper, or in a new document.

Students demonstrate contextual understanding of Benchmark Vocabulary. Students read text closely and use text evidence in their written answers.

Name ______________________________

Writing

Informative/Explanatory Writing: Use Precise Language and Domain-Specific Terms Use your notes from the research you conducted to write several paragraphs that inform about a special building or monument in your community or one that you have visited. Use precise language that includes words with positive connotations, define a key domain-specific term or concept from the lesson, and use formal language to describe the structure. Write your paragraphs on a separate sheet of paper or start a new document.

Conventions

Adjectives and Linking Verbs

DIRECTIONS Circle the linking verb and underline the predicate adjective in each sentence.

1. The Irish monument Knowth is fascinating.
2. The purpose of the monument became ceremonial.
3. The monument is peaceful from the outside.
4. The builders of Knowth were brilliant in science and astronomy.
5. The site, which includes one tomb and several smaller mounds, is enormous.
6. "To me, an artist," Collen said, "Knowth seems mysterious, like a myth come to life."

Students write routinely for a range of tasks, purposes, and audiences. Students practice various conventions of standard English.

Name ______________________________

Word Relationships: Synonyms and Antonyms

DIRECTIONS Find and write two synonyms in each sentence. Circle the signal words.

1. Farjana dislikes cleaning the family room because it is disorganized, or in other words, messy. ____________________
2. My brother will forsake his plan, as he must quit the race. ____________________
3. We expected Ian to be remorseful and say that he was sorry about being late. ____________________
4. Evan was diligent at his schoolwork, and his hardworking efforts led to his success. ____________________

DIRECTIONS Write two antonyms of the underlined word in each sentence. Circle the signal words.

5. Sam has <u>extravagant</u> tastes, although you wouldn't know that by looking at his plain and modest dorm room. ____________________
6. Eva always seemed <u>tranquil</u>, but the rest of her family was often wild and excitable. ____________________
7. Aidan made a <u>rookie</u> mistake on the experiment even though he was an experienced and qualified chemist. ____________________
8. The coach had <u>disregard</u> for the athlete's habit of showing up late, yet he had respect for her determination and felt appreciation for her skills. ____________________

DIRECTIONS Write the contrasting synonym/antonym pair. Circle the signal word that connects them.

9. Although student council members are in discord, we expect full agreement from them on this plan. ____________________
10. The prisoner acted as though he cherished the guard's kindness, yet he resented the man bitterly. ____________________
11. I relish most kinds of desserts; however, I do dislike cheesecake. ____________________
12. We obscured the smell with air freshener, but the scorched pan in the sink showed our parents that someone had burned dinner. ____________________

Students apply grade-level word analysis skills.

Name ______________________________

Benchmark Vocabulary

DIRECTIONS Write a sentence using each word.

urban sectors practical

Write in Response to Reading

Reread the last paragraph on page 52 of *Machu Picchu*. Using information from the text and illustrations, explain why the author describes Machu Picchu as a "special place" and its residents as having a "protected, holy existence."

Students demonstrate contextual understanding of Benchmark Vocabulary. Students read text closely and use text evidence in their written answers.

Name ____

Integrate Information

DIRECTIONS Using evidence from the text, answer the following questions about pages 46–53 from *Machu Picchu.*

1. The first two paragraphs on page 46 describe features that Machu Picchu had in common with other Inka towns. How does the painting on pages 46–47 further illustrate those similarities?

____

____

____

2. Reread the text on page 48. How does this text and the illustration on page 49 show the importance of the Sun Temple to Inka life?

____

____

____

3. How does the illustration on page 53 support the idea that the *panaka* members lived luxuriously in Machu Picchu?

____

____

____

4. How do the illustrations of people on pages 50 and 53 show the different levels of Inka society?

____

____

____

____

Students analyze and respond to literary and informational text.

Name ______________________________

Writing

Informative/Explanatory Writing: Write a Conclusion Review the paragraphs you wrote in Lesson 11. Then write a conclusion that summarizes the paragraphs. Make sure that you restate the topic and central idea, summarize key points from paragraphs you wrote, and give the reader a parting thought related to your topic. Write your conclusion on a separate sheet of paper or add it to your Lesson 11 paragraphs.

Conventions

Adverbs

DIRECTIONS Circle the adverb(s) and underline the word(s) modified in the sentences below.

1. Fort Ligonier in western Pennsylvania was built quickly during the French and Indian War.
2. France and Great Britain fought violently for control of North America.
3. France had erected Fort Duquesne at the strategically important Ohio River, where Pittsburgh stands today.
4. The British built an unusually large fort 50 miles east of Fort Duquesne.
5. They fought off a French attack and then marched west to occupy Fort Duquesne.
6. When our class toured Fort Ligonier, I was extremely impressed by the cannon and other frighteningly large weapons.

Students write routinely for a range of tasks, purposes, and audiences. Students practice various conventions of standard English.

Name ______________________________

Benchmark Vocabulary

DIRECTIONS Write a sentence using each word.

abruptly exposed rivalry

____

____

____

____

____

____

Write in Response to Reading

Reread the account of the meeting between Francisco Pizarro and Emperor Atawalpa on pages 56 and 59 of *Machu Picchu*. Do you think Pizarro expected the Catholic priest to be successful in converting Atawalpa to Christianity? State your opinion, and support it with evidence from the text. Write your answer below, on a separate sheet of paper, or in a new document.

____

____

____

____

____

____

____

____

____

____

Students demonstrate contextual understanding of Benchmark Vocabulary. Students read text closely and use text evidence in their written answers.

Name ______________________________

Thunder, Lightning, and Thor

Did you ever wonder how the word *Thursday* got its name? Well, it was named for Thor, a god in ancient Norse mythology. *Thursday* means "Thor's day." You may not have heard of Thor, but he has some other connections to today's world. For instance, thorium is a silvery-white element and source of nuclear energy, and was named after Thor by a Swedish chemist. Movies, toys, comic books, and a video game feature Thor, and a U.S. Air Force missile propelled by a rocket engine is named after him.

What makes Thor so interesting? He was one of the most powerful and popular of the Norse gods. A red beard, muscled body, and steel armor make Thor look fierce, and he was a powerful warrior and protector. He battled giants and serpents and was also the god of thunder. People then, as today, looked for ways to explain phenomena in nature that affected their lives. The Norse people wondered what caused the jagged lightning bolts they saw and the booms of thunder they heard. Stories about Thor provided them with answers.

According to Norse myth, Thor had a hammer he called Mjolnir (MYAWL-nir). He rode through the sky in a wheeled chariot pulled by two goats.

When he hurled Mjolnir at an enemy, Thor never missed. Amazingly, after the hammer hit its target, it would return to him.

The Norse people believed that lightning flashed after Thor threw his hammer and that thunder crashed and rumbled as his chariot wheels sped through the sky.

Through the centuries, of course, scientists have come up with other explanations for lightning and thunder. Now we know that lightning occurs when electricity is released in the atmosphere. We understand that the rapid expansion and compression of the heated air around the lightning bolt causes thunder.

Meteorologists study the air around Earth in order to warn us about dangerous storms so we can seek shelter. The next time you see lightning, try this little trick to judge how close lightning is. (It has nothing to do with Thor's hammer or chariot!) Simply count the number of seconds between the flash of lightning and the first clap of thunder. Divide the number by five to get a rough estimate of how many miles away the storm is. It turns out that every five seconds equals about one mile.

Students read text closely to determine what the text says.

Name ______________________________

Sleuth Work

Gather Evidence Underline text details that show Thor's connections to today's world.

Gather Evidence: Extend Your Ideas Review the text details you underlined. Why do you think the author included these details? Discuss your ideas with a partner.

____

____

Ask Questions Write two questions you might ask about the Norse myth of Thor.

____

____

Ask Questions: Extend Your Ideas Use text evidence to write how the Norse people might respond to a question about why their ancestors had believed the stories about Thor.

____

____

Make Your Case Box the portion of text that provides a scientific explanation for thunder and lightning. How is this information more helpful than the mythological explanation? Explain your opinion.

____

____

Make Your Case: Extend Your Ideas Why do you think both of the explanations of lightning and thunder might be valuable? Use text evidence to support your opinion.

____

____

Students read text closely to determine what the text says.

Writing

Name ____

Informative/Explanatory Writing: Select and Research a Topic Plan and research an informative article about another culture, ancient or modern, other than an ancient Central or South American civilization. First, decide on a culture that you find interesting and then narrow a topic. Develop questions and keywords to use in search engines or card catalogs. Then, conduct research using reliable sources. As you read, paraphrase each idea or write each quotation on a separate note card and include the author's name and the page number where you found the information.

On a separate sheet of paper or a new document, create a reference list that includes the following: author, title, city of publication, publisher, year of publication, and/or Web site address and date you accessed the information.

____

____

____

____

Conventions

Degrees of Comparison: Adjectives

DIRECTIONS Use the adjective at the end of each sentence and write the appropriate comparative or superlative form on the line provided.

1. Carvings on tortoise shells and ox bones are among the examples of the _______ writing in the world. (old)

2. The writing on clay tablets of Sumer, in the Middle East, is __________ than many other ancient writings. (early)

3. One scientist said, "The ____________________ bone carvings I've ever seen are from Mongolia." (beautiful)

4. Both cultures used pictographs, which some experts say are __________________ to translate than written words. (difficult)

5. Many people think the Chinese bone carvings are __________________ than the Sumerian clay tablets. (famous)

6. The Sumerian clay tablets are among the museum's _____________________ items. (important)

Students write routinely for a range of tasks, purposes, and audiences. Students practice various conventions of standard English.

Name ______________________________

Benchmark Vocabulary

DIRECTIONS Write a sentence using each word.

primitive urban

____

____

Write in Response to Reading

Reread the first and second paragraphs on page 61 of *Machu Picchu*. Explain how the ideas in these paragraphs are developed and supported in previous sections of the text. Write your answer below, on a separate sheet of paper, or in a new document.

____

____

____

____

____

____

____

____

____

____

____

____

____

____

____

Students demonstrate contextual understanding of Benchmark Vocabulary. Students read text closely and use text evidence in their written answers.

Name ___

Analyze Structure

DIRECTIONS Using evidence from the text, answer the following questions about pages 20–63 from *Machu Picchu.*

1. Reread the last paragraph on page 29. How does this paragraph conclude the information that precedes it? How does this paragraph introduce the information that follows?

2. How does the painting of Machu Picchu on pages 46–47 connect to the rest of the selection?

3. How does the information about the Sun Temple on pages 48 and 49 connect with central ideas about the Inkas?

Students analyze and respond to literary and informational text.

Name ______________________________

Writing

Informative/Explanatory Writing: Organize Organize your notes from the previous lesson in a logical order and use them to create an outline. Use Roman numerals for main topics, capital letters for subtopics, and numbers followed by lowercase letters (if needed) for supporting details.

Use these guidelines as you organize your notes:

- Arrange your note cards in a logical order.
- Choose a strategy to organize your ideas.
- Create an outline with main ideas, subtopics, and supporting details.
- Note where you could include a map, photo, diagram, or illustration to convey information.

Write your outline on a separate sheet of paper or start a new document.

Conventions

Degrees of Comparison: Adverbs Write the correct form of the adverb on the line provided in each sentence.

1. The Inka Empire was founded several centuries _________ than the Maya kingdom. (late, later, latest)
2. The Maya government was _______________ well organized. (amazingly, more amazingly, most amazingly)
3. The Inkas carved stone _________________ than any other people in the ancient world. (skillfully, more skillfully, most skillfully)
4. Of all the Maya's food crops, beans grew ______________. (fast, faster, fastest)
5. Feather headdresses created by Inkas were __________________________ displayed of all the items at the museum exhibit. (beautifully, more beautifully, the most beautifully)

Students write routinely for a range of tasks, purposes, and audiences. Students practice various conventions of standard English.

Benchmark Vocabulary

Name ______________________________

DIRECTIONS Write a sentence using each word.

survive flourish self-sufficient

____
____
____
____
____
____

Write in Response to Reading

Reread pages 72–74, focusing on Quetzalcoatl's transformation into a tiny black ant. Do you think he was wise to make this transformation? Draw inferences about Quetzalcoatl's actions based on the text and what you already know. Then use details and examples from the text to support your answer. Write your answer below, on a separate sheet of paper, or in a new document.

____
____
____
____
____
____
____
____
____
____

Students demonstrate contextual understanding of Benchmark Vocabulary. Students read text closely and use text evidence in their written answers.

Name ______________________________

Draw Inferences

DIRECTIONS Using evidence from the text, answer the following questions about pages 64–74 of *Quetzalcoatl and the Maize*.

1. Reread pages 64–70. Based on conversations among the gods, draw inferences about why only Quetzalcoatl was interested in the welfare of the Aztec people.

____

____

____

2. An Aztec woman cries out for help at the beginning of the myth. Based on the text and your own knowledge, what can you infer about Quetzalcoatl's abilities as a creator?

____

____

____

3. What does the ant queen's questioning of Quetzalcoatl when he's disguised as an ant tell you about her?

____

____

____

4. Reread the conversation between Quetzalcoatl and the ant queen on pages 72–74. What can you infer about characteristics they might have in common?

____

____

____

Students analyze and respond to literary or informational text.

Name ______________________________

Writing

Informative/Explanatory Writing: Write a Draft Write a complete first draft of your informative article. Keep writing until you have finished drafting all of your notes into sentences, following your outline to organize your ideas and information. If you discover a better way of organizing your ideas as you draft, make note of it and continue getting your ideas written into sentences. Do not worry about making everything perfect at this stage.

Keep the following points in mind as you write:

- Make sure your writing is appropriate for your purpose and audience.
- Keep your main ideas in a logical order and support them with sufficient details, including images, graphics, or multimedia materials.
- Maintain a formal writing style by being objective about your subject matter and including precise language and domain-specific vocabulary.

Write your draft on a separate sheet of paper or start a new document.

Conventions

Irregular Comparisons

DIRECTIONS Circle the incorrect adjective or adverb in each sentence and write the correct modifier on the line.

1. Roberta and I both think history is the better class of all. ___________
2. Of all ancient cultures, she knows less about the Inkas because she has not studied them in school. _________
3. My French is bad, but my Spanish is worst. _________
4. I am least good at track than I am at playing soccer. ___________

DIRECTIONS Write *adjective* or *adverb* on the line to identify the underlined word in each sentence.

1. You wrote your article well. ___________
2. His was the best article of all. ___________
3. I feel worse than I did yesterday. ___________

Students write routinely for a range of tasks, purposes, and audiences. Students practice various conventions of standard English.

Name ______________________________

Benchmark Vocabulary

DIRECTIONS Write a sentence using each word.

observant deceived

____

____

____

____

Write in Response to Reading

Reread page 79 of *Quetzalcoatl and the Maize*. Focus on Quetzalcoatl's realization that he must draw on contributions from multiple sources to solve his problem. What does this event reveal about Quetzalcoatl and the theme of the story? Use details and examples from the text to support your answer. Write your answer below, on a separate sheet of paper, or in a new document.

____

____

____

____

____

____

____

____

____

____

____

____

Students demonstrate contextual understanding of Benchmark Vocabulary. Students read text closely and use text evidence in their written answers.

Name ______________________________

Writing

Informative/Explanatory Writing: Review and Revise Review and revise the first draft of your informative article. You might need to revise some parts two or three times before you get the best wording and order of ideas, the best supporting details, and the best graphics. Use a separate sheet of paper or start a new document.

Keep the following points in mind as you revise:

- Ideas are clearly stated, supported, and flow in a logical order with the aid of transitions.
- Graphics support written ideas or show what would take several sentences to explain.
- All facts, examples, and supporting details are focused on the topic.
- The style is formal, avoiding judgments, opinions, and informal language (personal comments, slang, and contractions).

Conventions

Avoiding Double Comparisons

DIRECTIONS: Circle the incorrect comparison in each sentence and write the correct comparison on the lines provided.

1. The country of Mali in West Africa has existed more longer than most countries. ________
2. No one worked more harder to unite many tribes than the emperor Sundiata Keita in 1235 CE. ________
3. Mali had some of the most biggest gold and silver mines on the whole continent. ________
4. Another of ancient Mali's most valuablest resources was salt. ________
5. Mali's Emperor Musa was the most wealthiest person who ever lived in the country. ________
6. Musa loaded 200 camels with the most largest amount of gold and silver ever seen in a caravan. ________

Students write routinely for a range of tasks, purposes, and audiences. Students practice various conventions of standard English.

Name ______________________________

Connotation and Denotation

Word Bank

howl	protect	persistent	glare	inexpensive
childish	cultured	strategy	thrifty	terrorist

DIRECTIONS Write a word from the word bank that could complete each word pair, and identify whether it has a positive or negative connotation.

1. look ____________________

2. cry ____________________

3. stubborn ________________________

4. cheap ____________________

5. defend ____________________

6. snob ____________________

7. freedom fighter ____________________

8. penny-pinching ____________________

9. youthful ____________________

10. scheme ____________________

DIRECTIONS Write *neutral, positive,* or *negative* to tell the connotation of the underlined word.

11. small, scanty, <u>petite</u> __________

12. <u>secret</u>, confidential, concealed _________

13. grin, <u>smirk</u>, smile __________

14. slick, <u>smart</u>, ingenious _________

15. stench, smell, <u>aroma</u> __________

Students apply grade-level word analysis skills.

Benchmark Vocabulary

Name ______________________

DIRECTIONS Write a sentence using each word.

orderly dominate supreme

____

____

____

____

____

____

Write in Response to Reading

Reread pages 55–59 of *Machu Picchu* and pages 36–41 of *The Ancient Maya*. Use text evidence to write an informative/explanatory paragraph that compares and contrasts the decline of the Inka and the Maya civilizations. Write your answer below, on a separate sheet of paper, or in a new document.

____

____

____

____

____

____

____

____

____

____

Students demonstrate contextual understanding of Benchmark Vocabulary. Students read text closely and use text evidence in their written answers.

Name ____________________

Writing

Informative/Explanatory Writing: Edit and Proofread You will now edit and proofread the revised drafts you wrote for your informative article about an ancient culture. Use the following steps:

- Read through the article two or three times, sentence by sentence.
- Edit to choose the best wording to clearly explain ideas, making sure that you are using a formal style throughout.
- Identify and correct grammatical and mechanical errors.
- Identify and correct errors in spelling and punctuation.

Write the final version of your article on a separate sheet of paper or start a new document.

Conventions

Spell Correctly

DIRECTIONS Circle the misspelled word or words in each sentence and write the correct spellings on the lines provided. You may use a digital or online dictionary.

1. The amazeing Sumerians were among the first cultures to have schools, codes of law, and epic literature. ____________
2. The clay tablets that tell the storys of their lifes were lost for senturies.
   ____
3. A breif look at Sumer's history reveals a surprizingly modern way of life.
   ____
4. Archaeologists say the clay tabletes contain everything from sales reeseats to love letters. ____________
5. I would find it unpleasunt to write by drawing cimbals on clay. ____________

Students write routinely for a range of tasks, purposes, and audiences. Students practice various conventions of standard English.

Name ______________________________

Benchmark Vocabulary

DIRECTIONS Write a sentence using each word.

decline genius practical

Write in Response to Reading

Reread Chapter 2 of *The Ancient Maya* and pages 37–48 of *Machu Picchu*. Write paragraphs that compare and contrast the central idea that religion played an important role in the lives of these two civilizations. Use details and examples from the text to support your answer. Write your answer below, on a separate sheet of paper, or in a new document.

Students demonstrate contextual understanding of Benchmark Vocabulary. Students read text closely and use text evidence in their written answers.

Name ______________________________

Reading Analysis

Compare and Contrast

DIRECTIONS Using evidence from the text, answer the following questions about *The Ancient Maya*, "Secret to Mayan Blue Paint Found," *Machu Picchu*, and *Quetzalcoatl and the Maize*.

1. Reread pages 4–5 in *The Ancient Maya* and page 85 in "Secret to Mayan Blue Paint Found." How do the texts differ in presenting details about Mayan religious sacrifice?

____

____

____

2. Reread page 37 in *Machu Picchu* and pages 71 and 74 in *Quetzalcoatl and the Maize*. How does the informational text differ from the myth in conveying ideas about conquered peoples and religious acceptance?

____

____

____

____

3. How are ideas about history presented differently in *Machu Picchu*, *The Ancient Maya*, and *Quetzalcoatl and the Maize?*

____

____

____

____

____

4. How is the theme of self-sufficiency presented in *The Ancient Maya* compared to *Quetzalcoatl and the Maize*?

____

____

____

Students analyze and respond to literary and informational text.

Name ______________________

Writing

Informative/Explanatory Writing: Publish and Present Now you will format, publish, and present your article about an ancient culture. Limit your presentation to the allotted time. As you publish and present your writing, keep the following points in mind:

- Select a format and place images and/or multimedia materials next to key points to clarify the text.
- Choose a print or digital option to publish the article.
- In your oral presentation, make good eye contact; speak clearly and loud enough to be heard; and use formal, standard English.

Write the final version of your informative article on a separate sheet of paper or start a new document.

Conventions

Use Standard English

DIRECTIONS: Rewrite each sentence on the line in formal, standard English.

1. Ancient cultures are super fascinating. Anyways, studying them is like time travel.

____

2. Ancient Rome with all its gladiator fights is a whole nother story.

____

3. The huge stones been cut, and the Inka hauled those guys up the steep trails.

____

4. We've got heavy machinery today, but we ain't able to build monuments like the ones at Machu Picchu.

____

____

Students write routinely for a range of tasks, purposes, and audiences. Students practice various conventions of standard English.

Name ______________________________

Benchmark Vocabulary

DIRECTIONS Write a sentence using each word.

predict severe destructive

____

____

____

____

____

____

Write in Response to Reading

Reread the section "Ocean currents" on page 9 and look at the map. Write a paragraph that explains what ocean currents are and what causes them. Write your response below, on a separate sheet of paper, or in a new document.

____

____

____

____

____

____

Students demonstrate contextual understanding of Benchmark Vocabulary. Students read text closely and use text evidence in their written answers.

Name ______________________

Writing

Argument Writing: Identify Purpose and Structure of an Argument The selection *Ocean Storm Alert!* explains how weather and climate can affect communities close to an ocean. Write two claims about the effect of weather and climate on human populations using evidence from the text. Use a separate sheet of paper or start a new document.

Conventions

Form and Use Gerunds

DIRECTIONS Rewrite the sentences below by using gerunds to replace the underlined words.

1. To watch the skies helps sailors predict an ocean storm.

2. Floods may happen because of the rise of water levels.

3. Evaporation occurs with the heat of water.

4. To take shelter during a storm is a wise idea.

5. The captain supports the build of a reinforced ship.

Students write routinely for a range of tasks, purposes, and audiences. Students practice various conventions of standard English.

Name ______________________________

Shades of Meaning

DIRECTIONS: Read each set of words and consider the meaning of each. Use a dictionary to determine or clarify meanings. Write the words in order of degree of intensity from least to most. Then write a sentence for each word that clearly illustrates its shade of meaning and distinguishes it from the other two words.

shameful, embarrassing, humiliating ______________________________

1. ______________________________

2. ______________________________

3. ______________________________

puzzled, confused, stumped ______________________________

4. ______________________________

5. ______________________________

6. ______________________________

peculiar, extraordinary, odd ______________________________

7. ______________________________

8. ______________________________

9. ______________________________

warily, carefully, gingerly ______________________________

10. ______________________________

11. ______________________________

12. ______________________________

Students apply grade-level word analysis skills.

Name ______________________________

Benchmark Vocabulary

DIRECTIONS Write a sentence using each word.

vulnerable collide monitors

Write in Response to Reading

Reread pages 10–11 and look at the maps. Write an opinion paragraph that tells where in the world you think storms pose the most danger to people and why. Write your answer below, on a separate sheet of paper, or in a new document.

Students demonstrate contextual understanding of Benchmark Vocabulary. Students read text closely and use text evidence in their written answers.

Name ___________________________________

Compare and Contrast to Evaluate Information

DIRECTIONS Using evidence from the text, answer the following questions about *Ocean Storm Alert!*

1. Based on the information about whirlpools on page 15, compare and contrast the Maelstrom to the whirlpool shown in the photo.

____

____

____

____

____

2. Compare and contrast the effects of rogue waves and whirlpools on ships.

____

____

____

____

____

3. What is the difference between a hurricane and a tropical storm?

____

____

____

____

4. How are storm surges similar to waterspouts? How are they different?

____

____

____

____

Students analyze and respond to literary and informational text.

Name ______________________________

Writing

Argument Writing: Gather and Analyze Text Evidence In *Ocean Storm Alert!* the author explains that ocean waters present serious dangers to human populations. Based on your notes, write a paragraph summarizing the key ideas in the selection. Use the space below, or write your paragraph on a separate sheet of paper.

Conventions

Form and Use Participles

DIRECTIONS Read each sentence. Change the verb in parentheses to the correct past or present participle. Write the new sentence below.

1. The (rush) monsoon winds blow the ship across the sea.

2. Rescuers helped the men out of the (wreck) ship.

3. After the storm, they will replace the (break) windows.

4. The (surge) waves of a tsunami can destroy a town.

Students write routinely for a range of tasks, purposes, and audiences. Students practice various conventions of standard English.

Name ______________________________

Benchmark Vocabulary

DIRECTIONS Write a sentence using each word.

catastrophic   approximately   detected

____

____

____

____

____

____

Write in Response to Reading

Reread the section "Disasters at Sea" on pages 20–21. Select one of the shipwrecks described and write a paragraph that gives your opinion on which wreck would be the most interesting to explore. Use details from the text to support your opinion. Write your answer below, on a separate sheet of paper, or in a new document.

____

____

____

____

____

____

Students demonstrate contextual understanding of Benchmark Vocabulary. Students read text closely and use text evidence in their written answers.

Name ______________________________

Are You Thinking About a Survival Camp?

If you've ever wanted to escape the routine of your everyday life to try something new, then a weekend survival camp might be just the thing. What would convince city dwellers to venture into the wilderness for 48 hours? Well, different people have different reasons. Some are curious to try new sports, such as rafting, rock climbing, kayaking, canoeing, and fishing. Others want to learn survival skills like building a shelter and finding food and water. Still others wish to test themselves, physically and mentally, in an unpredictable and rugged environment.

Most wilderness survival programs have age and health requirements for participants. Some organizations have designed weekends especially for 12- and 13-year-olds. Some of these programs require campers to carry all their equipment in a backpack. That includes food, clothing, and tents. Each day campers hike to a different campsite that the leaders have scouted out in advance. Everyone keeps active with games, sports, and team-building exercises. Wilderness weekends generally emphasize problem solving, physical fitness, and just plain fun. Some wilderness camps are now adding opportunities for campers to explore nature and improve the environment. Campers work under a ranger's supervision to help restore and maintain the natural habitat.

Of course, safety is always a major concern. Everyone must be prepared for the unexpected. Weather conditions can change quickly and dramatically, for example. In camps that stress survival skills, leaders and campers learn to identify water sources and edible plants in the area. Each group of hikers carries matches, a whistle or mirror for signaling, and a tin cup for heating food. Matches can be ruined by rain, so hikers practice how to create sparks by striking metal against rock or using a magnifying glass and energy from the sun. Above all, everybody learns the importance of staying calm in tough or uncertain situations.

Do weekend survival camps result in long-term benefits for young people? Do they help campers develop self-reliance, resourcefulness, or confidence—skills they can use when they return to their homes and daily routines? People certainly disagree about the answer to those questions. The truth is that not much research has been done on the long-term value and effects of wilderness camps on campers' lives. But for many people, a weekend getaway in the wilderness is an adventure of a lifetime.

Students read text closely to determine what the text says.

Name ______________________

Sleuth Work

Gather Evidence On page 111, underline the text details that explain why some students might enjoy survival camp.

Gather Evidence: Extend Your Ideas Review the reasons for enjoying survival camp. What specific activities are offered to students for two or more of these reasons?

____

____

____

____

Ask Questions Write two questions you might ask if you were considering attending a survival camp.

____

____

____

____

Ask Questions: Extend Your Ideas Choose one of the two questions you have about survival camps. Scan the text on page 111, and look for details that might suggest an answer to your question. Then write a follow-up question based on those details.

____

____

Make Your Case Put brackets around details that make a survival camp a good learning experience.

Make Your Case: Extend Your Ideas What would you be most excited about learning at a survival camp? Why? Use evidence from the text to explain your reasons.

____

____

____

Students read text closely to determine what the text says.

Name ______________________________

Writing

Argument Writing: State and Support A Claim *Ocean Storm Alert!* explores the dangers that ocean waters pose to people's safety. Write a claim and an introductory paragraph about this topic. Include relevant information from the text that directly supports your claim. Use the space below or a separate sheet of paper to write your introductory paragraph.

____

____

____

____

____

____

____

____

Conventions

Form and Use Infinitives

DIRECTIONS Write four sentences using an infinitive in each one. Vary your sentence structures to include the infinitive as the subject, subject complement, or direct object.

1. ____

____

2. ____

____

3. ____

____

4. ____

____

Students write routinely for a range of tasks, purposes, and audiences. Students practice various conventions of standard English.

Name ______________________________

Benchmark Vocabulary

DIRECTIONS Write a sentence using each word.

organizations coordinate artificial

____

____

____

____

____

____

Write in Response to Reading

Reread the section "After the Storm" on pages 28–29. Write a letter to community members who are recovering from the effects of a hurricane. In the letter, explain how others will help them rebuild their community. Use facts and information from the text in your letter. Write your letter below, on a separate sheet of paper, or in a new document.

____

____

____

____

____

____

____

____

____

____

Students demonstrate contextual understanding of Benchmark Vocabulary. Students read text closely and use text evidence in their written answers.

Name ______________________________

Writing

Argument Writing: Support a Claim with Clear Reasons and Relevant Evidence Create an outline for an essay about the biggest danger ocean waters pose to people's safety that will include an introduction, two body paragraphs, and a concluding paragraph. Remember to present the strongest evidence first. Use a separate sheet of paper or start a new document to write your outline.

Conventions

Maintain Subject-Verb Agreement with Noun Phrases

DIRECTIONS Write four sentences of your own. Include one or more sentences with a noun phrase that comes between the subject and the verb. Remember to check your sentences for correct subject-verb agreement.

1. ____

____

2. ____

____

3. ____

____

4. ____

____

Students write routinely for a range of tasks, purposes, and audiences. Students practice various conventions of standard English.

Name ______________________________

Benchmark Vocabulary

DIRECTIONS Write a sentence using this word.

buoyancy

____

____

Write in Response to Reading

Reread "Recipe for Disaster" on pages 30–31. Write a paragraph that gives your opinion about whether this is a good experiment to include at the end of *Ocean Storm Alert!* Support your opinion with details and evidence from the text. Write your paragraph below, on a separate sheet of paper, or in a new document.

____

____

____

____

____

____

____

____

____

____

____

Students demonstrate contextual understanding of Benchmark Vocabulary. Students read text closely and use text evidence in their written answers.

Name ____________________

Analyze Text and Visual Features

DIRECTIONS Using evidence from the text, answer the following questions about *Ocean Storm Alert!*

1. Look at the world map on page 9. How does it help you understand the text?

____

____

____

____

____

____

2. Explain your opinion on whether the map on page 9 is the best way to convey this information.

____

____

____

____

____

____

3. What questions do you have about currents that are not answered in this text feature? Write two questions.

____

____

____

____

____

____

Students analyze and respond to literary and informational text.

Name ______________________________

Writing

Argument Writing: Use Words, Phrases, and Clauses to Clarify Relationships Write a paragraph developing reasons or evidence that support your claim. Consider the following before writing:

- What transitional words or phrases can I use to connect my paragraphs?
- What is the relationship between my key idea and details?
- How can I smoothly flow from one sentence to the next?

Write your paragraph below or on a separate sheet of paper, or start a new document.

____

____

____

____

____

____

Conventions

Subject-Verb Agreement with Indefinite Pronouns

DIRECTIONS Complete the sentences below by circling the correct indefinite pronoun. Then write a sentence using an indefinite pronoun as the subject.

1. Anyone who has been in a hurricane (know / knows) how dangerous it is.
2. Most of the sailors (has / have) sailed through a hurricane.
3. The meteorologist makes sure that no one (forget / forgets) to prepare for a coming hurricane.
4. Whether a tsunami or hurricane approaches, both (cause / causes) destruction.
5. ______________________________
____

Students write routinely for a range of tasks, purposes, and audiences. Students practice various conventions of standard English.

Name ______________________________

Benchmark Vocabulary

DIRECTIONS Write a sentence using each word.

disturbance exceptionally expanding

____

____

____

____

____

____

Write in Response to Reading

Reread page 94 and look at the diagram. Write a paragraph explaining what the parts of a wave are and how a wave is measured. Use details from the text in your answer. Write your paragraph below, on a separate sheet of paper, or in a new document.

____

____

____

____

____

____

____

____

____

____

____

____

Students demonstrate contextual understanding of Benchmark Vocabulary. Students read text closely and use text evidence in their written answers.

Name ______________________________

Writing

Argument Writing: Establish and Maintain a Formal Style Review the claim and evidence in your outline and first body paragraph. Based on your outline and first body paragraph, write a second body paragraph on a separate sheet of paper or start a new document.

Conventions

Maintain Subject-Verb Agreement with Collective Nouns

DIRECTIONS Circle the verb that agrees with the collective noun in each sentence.

1. The team (win / wins) every game because the coach has a brilliant strategy.
2. The crew (take / takes) separate shifts steering the ship through the storm.
3. At dinnertime, our family (tell / tells) stories about interesting events.
4. A flock of seagulls (fly / flies) over the surfers waiting for a good ocean wave.
5. The band happily (play / plays) several songs for the growing audience.

Students write routinely for a range of tasks, purposes, and audiences. Students practice various conventions of standard English.

Name ______________________________

Word Analysis

Multiple-Meaning Words

DIRECTIONS Write the word from the Word Bank that best completes each sentence. Use each word twice. Write a definition for the word as it is used in the sentence. Use a dictionary as needed.

Word Bank

motion	volume	friction	culture	range

1. Scientists can __________ bacteria in a lab, using special substances to feed them.

   Definition: __________

2. The market received a large __________ of complaints about its overpriced vegetables.

   Definition: __________

3. It was getting late, and the mayor made a __________ to end the meeting.

   Definition: __________

4. There was __________ between management and the unhappy workers.

   Definition: __________

5. The teams in the paintball tournament must __________ throughout the woods that make up the course.

   Definition: __________

6. The __________ of rough sandpaper on wood can create heat.

   Definition: __________

7. When you come to a stop sign, all forward __________ of the car should stop before you move again.

   Definition: __________

8. The __________ of this bottle of water is two liters.

   Definition: __________

9. The Sierra Nevada is a mountain __________ in California and Nevada.

   Definition: __________

10. I am looking forward to studying the __________ of ancient Greece.

    Definition: __________

Students apply grade-level word analysis skills.

Name ________________________

Benchmark Vocabulary

DIRECTIONS Write a sentence using each word.

circulation triggering

____

____

____

____

Write in Response to Reading

Reread pages 96–97. Write a paragraph that gives your opinion about whether the explanation on these pages helps the reader better understand the discussion of tsunamis on pages 98–99. Use details from the text to support your opinion. Write your paragraph below, on a separate sheet of paper, or in a new document.

____

____

____

____

____

____

____

Students demonstrate contextual understanding of Benchmark Vocabulary. Students read text closely and use text evidence in their written answers.

Name ________________________________

Argument Writing: Assess Strength of Argument Review the introductory paragraph and two body paragraphs you have written for your argument. As you look over your draft, use the checklist you created to assess the strength of your argument. Then revise your draft until you are satisfied that it presents and supports a strong argument. Write your revised draft on a separate sheet of paper or start a new document.

Consider these questions as you evaluate your evidence:

- Are my reasons supported with relevant and accurate evidence from the text?
- Have I presented the strongest reasons and evidence first?
- Have I included factual evidence rather than personal opinion?
- Is any of my evidence weak or unrelated to my claim and reasons?

Subject-Verb Agreement in Inverted Sentences

DIRECTIONS Complete each sentence by circling the correct verb from the pair in parentheses. Then write two of your own inverted sentences. Remember to check for correct subject-verb agreement.

1. There (lies / lie) the pieces of a ship that was sunk in a terrible storm.

2. With the North Wind (comes / come) a blast of icy air.

3. Below the ocean's surface (is / are) many hidden secrets.

4. ________________________________

____

5. ________________________________

____

Students write routinely for a range of tasks, purposes, and audiences. Students practice various conventions of standard English.

Name ____________________

Benchmark Vocabulary

DIRECTIONS Write a sentence using each word.

source compresses particles

____

____

____

____

____

____

Write in Response to Reading

Choose an explanation about a concept in "Sound Waves" or "Light Waves" that you found effective. Write a few sentences paraphrasing the information provided by the author and then explain why you think the author's method helps readers understand the information. Write your answer below, on a separate sheet of paper, or in a new document.

____

____

____

____

____

____

____

____

Students demonstrate contextual understanding of Benchmark Vocabulary. Students read text closely and use text evidence in their written answers.

Name ______________________________

Analyze How Text Structure Conveys Purpose

DIRECTIONS Using evidence from the text, answer the following questions about pages 100–113 from *Waves: Energy on the Move*.

1. Why does the discussion of the Doppler effect fit in well with the other topics about sound waves?

____
____
____
____
____
____

2. Light and sound waves both affect our senses. What key difference between the two types of waves makes it sensible to explore them in separate chapters?

____
____
____
____
____
____

Students analyze and respond to literary and informational text.

Name ____

Writing

Argument Writing: Write an Effective Conclusion Review your argument essay. As you look over your draft, highlight or make notes about your key points so that you can briefly summarize them in your concluding paragraph. Then think about how you will add new insight. Choose one of these ideas to include in the conclusion:

- a question causing readers to reflect on the argument
- a recommendation for readers in response to the argument
- an informational statement to explain why the topic and your claim is important

Remember to use transitional words or phrases to link your conclusion to the previous paragraph in your essay. Use a separate sheet of paper or start a new document to write your conclusion.

Conventions

Use Prepositions and Prepositional Phrases

DIRECTIONS Underline the prepositional phrases in sentences 1 and 2. Then write three sentences containing prepositional phrases. Remember to choose appropriate prepositions for each phrase you write.

1. Use the elevator in the east wing for your wheelchair.
2. Ask the staff in the office to draw you a map of the ground floor.
3. ____
____
4. ____
____
5. ____
____

Students write routinely for a range of tasks, purposes, and audiences. Students practice various conventions of standard English.

Name ______________________________

Benchmark Vocabulary

DIRECTIONS Write a sentence using each word.

communications assigned vary

Write in Response to Reading

The central idea in the chapter "Earthquake Waves" is that seismic waves are very powerful. Write a paragraph summarizing the details that support this idea. Write your answer below, on a separate sheet of paper, or in a new document.

Students demonstrate contextual understanding of Benchmark Vocabulary. Students read text closely and use text evidence in their written answers.

Name ____________________

Writing

Argument Writing: Analyze Purpose and Audience Reread page 126 of *Waves: Energy on the Move*. Use text evidence to form a claim that states the author's purpose and intended audience for the selection. Write a paragraph stating and supporting your claim with reasons and text evidence. Use a separate sheet of paper or start a new document to write your paragraph.

Conventions

Use Object Pronouns with Prepositions

DIRECTIONS Complete the sentences below using a pronoun that correctly completes the second sentence in each pair.

1. During the storm, Maya was calmly reassuring to her pets. She realized that the crashing thunder was frightening to ________________.

2. A tornado funnel appeared as Andy was walking home. The sky above ________________ grew dense and black.

3. The earthquake shook the house in the field. The ground beneath ________________ began to split apart.

4. Lena wandered through San Francisco. She noticed that the buildings around ________________ were built to withstand earthquakes.

5. We heard the neighbor's dog barking behind the fence. I told my sister, "I think the dog is barking at ________________, not me."

6. After the hurricane, a journalist came to our house. She asked if she could write an article about ________________ and our house.

Students write routinely for a range of tasks, purposes, and audiences. Students practice various conventions of standard English.

Benchmark Vocabulary

Name ______________________________

DIRECTIONS Write a sentence using the word.

stems

____

____

Write in Response to Reading

Now that you have read the entire text, *Waves: Energy on the Move,* think about a fact from pages 95–131 that you found especially surprising or interesting. In your own words, explain the fact and write about how the author presented the information in an interesting way.

____

____

____

____

____

____

____

____

____

____

____

____

____

____

____

Students demonstrate contextual understanding of Benchmark Vocabulary. Students read text closely and use text evidence in their written answers.

Name ______________________________

Analyze Text and Visual Features

DIRECTIONS Using evidence from the text, answer the following questions about *Waves: Energy on the Move*.

1. The Ring of Fire is an area in the Pacific Ocean with active underwater volcanoes and earthquakes. How does the map on page 125 serve as a good visual representation of the Ring of Fire?

____

____

____

____

2. What images in *Waves: Energy on the Move* appeal to readers' emotions? What point of view does the author convey with these images?

____

____

____

____

3. How do the "Did You Know?" text features throughout the book help the author communicate her purpose?

____

____

____

____

Students analyze and respond to literary and informational text.

Name ____________________

Writing

Argument Writing: Revise an Argument Essay Review the draft you wrote about the biggest threat to people's safety posed by ocean waters. Revise your essay to express your own point of view about this topic. Make your revisions on a separate sheet of paper or start a new document.

Conventions

Differentiate Prepositions and Adverbs

DIRECTIONS Write four sentences or pairs of sentences in which you use the same word as both a preposition and an adverb.

1. ____________________

2. ____________________

3. ____________________

4. ____________________

Students write routinely for a range of tasks, purposes, and audiences. Students practice various conventions of standard English.

Name ______________________________

Benchmark Vocabulary

DIRECTIONS Write a sentence using each word.

catastrophic detected disturbance

____

____

____

____

____

____

Write in Response to Reading

Both *Ocean Storm Alert!* and *Waves: Energy on the Move* use visual features to explain concepts in the text. Examine the visual on page 14 of *Ocean Storm Alert!* and page 99 of *Waves: Energy on the Move.* Write a paragraph comparing and contrasting the authors' use of the visual features.

____

____

____

____

____

____

____

____

____

____

____

Students demonstrate contextual understanding of Benchmark Vocabulary. Students read text closely and use text evidence in their written answers.

Name ______________________________

Writing

Argument Writing: Evaluate Pros and Cons Reread the sections "Monster Waves" on pages 14–15 from *Ocean Storm Alert!* and "Tsunami, a Killer Wave" on pages 98–99 from *Waves: Energy on the Move*. Compare and contrast the accounts of a tsunami. Once you have made a judgment about which text was most effective, write a claim. In your claim, use language such as *least effective, most advantageous, worst,* or *best.*

____

____

____

____

____

Conventions

Use Coordinating Conjunctions

DIRECTIONS Write four sentences, using the directions below. Remember to use the coordinating conjunction that best fits the meaning of each of your sentences.

1. Use a coordinating conjunction to create a compound subject.

____

____

2. Use a coordinating conjunction to create a compound predicate.

____

____

3. Use a coordinating conjunction to create a compound object.

____

____

4. Use a coordinating conjunction to create a compound sentence.

____

____

Students write routinely for a range of tasks, purposes, and audiences. Students practice various conventions of standard English.

Name ______________________________

Greek and Latin Prefixes *non-, post-, super-, hyper-, para-*

non-: not, without
post-: after
super-: over, above, beyond
hyper-: over, above, excessively
para-: alongside, beyond

DIRECTIONS Write the word from the Word Bank that has the same meaning as the phrase.

Word Bank

postwar	superhighway	nondairy	nonflammable	paralegal
nonprofit	postmodern	hyperspace	superhuman	postscript

1. not containing or made with milk 1. ______________
2. related to an era after the current one 2. ______________
3. not burning or not burning easily 3. ______________
4. greater than normal power or size 4. ______________
5. without intent of financial gain 5. ______________
6. happening after a conflict 6. ______________

DIRECTIONS Use a word from the Word Bank to complete each sentence.

7. In a science fiction story, I read about ______________, where alien craft travel faster than the speed of light.
8. The lawyer was looking for a ______________ to assist her with the case.
9. A new ______________ was built to provide more roads for the heavy traffic between cities.
10. He didn't write about his new job in the body of the letter, but he mentioned it in the ______________.

Students apply grade-level word analysis skills.

Name ______________________________

Benchmark Vocabulary

DIRECTIONS Write a sentence using each word.

predict   destructive   communications

Write in Response to Reading

Waves are powerful forces that can cause great damage. Reread pages 20–21 of *Ocean Storm Alert!* and page 121 of *Waves: Energy on the Move*. Write a paragraph analyzing the words and phrases each author uses to communicate a sense of danger.

Students demonstrate contextual understanding of Benchmark Vocabulary. Students read text closely and use text evidence in their written answers.

Name ______________________________

Word Choice

DIRECTIONS Using evidence from the text, answer the following questions about *Ocean Storm Alert!* and *Waves: Energy on the Move*.

1. The author of *Ocean Storm Alert!* has to describe the movement of waves over and over again. What are some of the words she uses to vary the language about movement throughout the book?

____

____

____

____

2. Why does the author of *Waves: Energy on the Move* include the information about singer Enrico Caruso on p. 126?

____

____

____

____

3. What language does the author of *Waves: Energy on the Move* use to help readers understand the terrible effect of earthquakes?

____

____

____

____

Students analyze and respond to literary and informational text.

Name ______________________

Writing

Argument Writing: Engage Audience Before you begin to write, think about some descriptive words and examples of figurative language to include in your draft. Then write two body paragraphs and a conclusion in which you incorporate your descriptions and figurative language.

Conventions

Use Correlative Conjunctions

DIRECTIONS Rewrite each pair of sentences below by joining the sentences with correlative conjunctions. Remember, correlative conjunctions come in pairs.

1. A swamp is a likely place to spot alligators. A lagoon is also a likely place to spot alligators.

____

____

2. The canal is frequently used for boating. It is also used for fishing.

____

____

3. We did not hear the high-pitched whistle. We did not hear the low-pitched whistle.

____

____

4. Engineers will build a structure that can withstand an earthquake. It will also withstand a tsunami.

____

____

5. You can have an apple for lunch. You can have a sandwich for lunch.

____

____

Students write routinely for a range of tasks, purposes, and audiences. Students practice various conventions of standard English.

Name ______________________________

Benchmark Vocabulary

DIRECTIONS Write a sentence using each word.

generating conservation efficiency

____

____

____

____

____

____

Write in Response to Reading

Reread the last two paragraphs on page 133 and the next three paragraphs on page 134 of "Offshore Wind Still the Best Bet for Clean Energy." Briefly summarize the author's reasons why these alternate sources of renewable energy are impractical for the state of Massachusetts. Then explain whether the author has convinced you that offshore wind farms are the best way to generate power in Massachusetts. Write your answer below, on a separate sheet of paper, or in a new document.

____

____

____

____

____

____

____

____

____

____

Students demonstrate contextual understanding of Benchmark Vocabulary. Students read text closely and use text evidence in their written answers.

Name ____

Wilderness Medic

In her teens, Sasha decided that a desk job wasn't for her. But what was? Sitting in health class one day, she became curious when Manolo, a paramedic, described his experiences being the first to respond when people are injured. He shared stories of car crashes, fires, tornadoes, and other emergencies.

When someone asked, "With all the risks, why do you do it?" Manolo paused for a minute. "First, nothing is better than seeing that you made a difference, having people express their gratitude that you were there for them during a tough time. Second, someone needs to do this work. I have a great job, and I love it, so why not me?"

Intrigued, Sasha began researching the requirements to become a paramedic. She learned that she had to undergo a lot of medical training and also be able to successfully deal with difficult and stressful situations. Paramedics have to be confident leaders who can quickly assess a situation, make decisions under pressure, and take action to stabilize a patient. They must remain calm, even in situations that may include violence or danger.

Sasha loved the outdoors and physical challenges, so after earning her certification, she went on to become a wilderness paramedic. She had dealt with wounds, burns, fractures, infections, heart attacks, and spinal cord injuries in the city, but that was with a well-equipped ambulance. Now, she had to learn to do similar things after being lowered by a helicopter into thick woods or onto a snowy mountain in extreme temperatures. She had to carry everything she needed, often pushing her body to its limits. During the difficult moments she remembered Manolo's words. *Somebody needs to do this work*. And like Manolo, Sasha knew that this job was her special destiny, and she excelled at it.

Finally, her first call came as a wilderness medic! A hiker who had slipped off the trail and fallen onto a rocky ledge was conscious but couldn't move. As the helicopter approached the scene, Sasha's mind raced, but as she maneuvered down the rope to the injured hiker, she remained calm. She heard the man's friends screaming down from the trail and saw the panicked look on the hiker's face. Sasha knelt down and gave him her hand. "I'm here to help you; just stay calm," she whispered quietly in his ear. She knew she had the skills to keep that promise.

Students read text closely to determine what the text says.

Name ____________________

Gather Evidence On page 139, underline text details that show the physical challenges that wilderness medics face.

Gather Evidence: Extend Your Ideas Read through the text you underlined. What kind of person would enjoy the physical challenges that come with being a wilderness medic?

____

____

____

Ask Questions Write a question you have for Sasha about her physical training as a wilderness medic.

____

____

____

Ask Questions: Extend Your Ideas Read through the last paragraph of the text. What question could you ask about how Sasha was able to help the injured hiker?

____

____

____

Make Your Case Did Sasha make a good decision about her career? Use text evidence to support your opinion.

____

____

____

Make Your Case: Extend Your Ideas Connect Sasha's experience at the end with the information about wilderness medics earlier in the text.

____

____

____

Students read text closely to determine what the text says.

Name ______________________________

Writing

Argument Writing: Gather Evidence for a Persuasive Speech Review *Waves: Energy on the Move* and determine which type of wave is most worthy of further study by scientists. Then gather text evidence supporting your argument about which wave scientists should study. Use a separate sheet of paper or start a new document to record your evidence.

Conventions

Use Subordinating Conjunctions

DIRECTIONS Using a subordinating conjunction, rewrite the pairs of sentences below as a single sentence. Then write two of your own sentences using subordinating conjunctions.

1. Astronomers can now learn about the deepest parts of space. They have powerful telescopes.

____

____

2. Albert Einstein proved that light could behave as a particle. He made an important discovery.

____

____

3. ______________________________

____

4. ______________________________

____

Students write routinely for a range of tasks, purposes, and audiences. Students practice various conventions of standard English.

Name ______________________________

Benchmark Vocabulary

DIRECTIONS Write a sentence using each word.

theme resourceful renewable

Write in Response to Reading

The individual brainstorming scene on pages 13–16 of *Science Fair Showdown!* gives readers glimpses into all three main characters' thoughts. Briefly rewrite the scene from the first-person point of view of one of the three characters.

Students demonstrate contextual understanding of Benchmark Vocabulary. Students read text closely and use text evidence in their written answers.

Name ______________________________

Analyze Narrative Point of View

DIRECTIONS Using evidence from the text, answer the following questions about pages 4–18 from *Science Fair Showdown!*

1. What is the main conflict in the story so far? What additional obstacles do we learn about through the narrator?

2. How would there be less conflict in this story if the students entered the science fair individually?

3. What conflicts do you predict will surface for the friends as the story goes on? What information in the first two chapters makes you think that?

Students analyze and respond to literary and informational text.

Name ____

Writing

Argument Writing: Plan a Persuasive Speech Write a claim about which type of wave needs further scientific study. Develop an outline organizing the key points of your argument. Think about which reasons support your claim and make a plan to develop the reasons with evidence in the body paragraphs of a persuasive speech. Remember to use relevant facts and details from *Waves: Energy on the Move* as you create your outline. Write your claim and outline on a separate sheet of paper or start a new document.

Conventions

Use Independent Clauses

DIRECTIONS Write a complete clause by adding either a subject or predicate to the groups of words below. Then write two independent clauses of your own. Use either a compound subject or a compound predicate in one of your new sentences.

1. My classmates, Kai and Rosa, ____

____.

2. ______________________________ observed and applauded their efforts.

3. ____

____

4. ____

____

Students write routinely for a range of tasks, purposes, and audiences. Students practice various conventions of standard English.

Name ______________________________

Benchmark Vocabulary

DIRECTIONS Write a sentence using each word.

portable convert enthusiasm

Write in Response to Reading

In Chapter 3, the narrator of *Science Fair Showdown!* describes the three main characters as they go home to work on their ideas. What details does the writer use to show what their lives are like outside of school? Choose two of the characters and compare and contrast their lives at home.

Students demonstrate contextual understanding of Benchmark Vocabulary. Students read text closely and use text evidence in their written answers.

Name ________________________________

Writing

Argument Writing: Draft a Persuasive Speech Review your outline. Draft a persuasive speech using the plan written in your outline. In the introductory paragraph, state your claim and main reasons to support this claim. Then develop your reasons in the body paragraphs and summarize your argument in the conclusion. Focus on supporting your claim with evidence using first-person point of view without bias. Write your draft on a separate sheet of paper or start a new document.

Conventions

Connect Independent Clauses

DIRECTIONS Connect the pairs of independent clauses below by using a comma and the conjunction *and*, *but*, or *or*. Be sure to choose the conjunction that shows a logical relationship of ideas. Rewrite the sentences in the space provided.

1. The lighthouses used in earlier times employed keepers. Today's lighthouses are often automated.

   ____

   ____

2. A lighthouse keeper could fuel his lamps with oil. He could use kerosene for this purpose.

   ____

   ____

3. Lighthouses can guide ships through dangerous waters. They help boats navigate through fog.

   ____

   ____

4. Some old lighthouses are no longer in use. Tourists like to visit them.

   ____

   ____

Students write routinely for a range of tasks, purposes, and audiences. Students practice various conventions of standard English.

Name ____________________

Benchmark Vocabulary

DIRECTIONS Write a sentence using each word.

competition critical alternative

Write in Response to Reading

Principal Sanchez wants Albert, Sofia, and Diya to serve on a committee about using renewable energy at the school. Write your opinion on whether the three students would make good consultants for the committee. Use details from the text to support your opinion.

Students demonstrate contextual understanding of Benchmark Vocabulary. Students read text closely and use text evidence in their written answers.

Name ______________________________

Writing

Argument Writing: Revise a Persuasive Speech Review your draft to determine the effectiveness of your argument about the type of waves that deserve further scientific study. Use this checklist to make sure your argument is sound.

- strong reasons and evidence to support the claim and reasons
- connection of ideas with words and phrases
- meaning of content and domain-specific words is clear to the audience
- language that interests and engages the audience

Make sure you use language that strengthens your claims and engages the audience. Make your revisions on a separate sheet of paper or start a new document.

Conventions

Identify Dependent Clauses

DIRECTIONS Underline the dependent clause in each sentence below. Then write two of your own sentences using a subordinating conjunction to join a dependent and an independent clause. Remember to use a comma if the dependent clause comes before the independent clause in the sentence.

1. When earthquakes occur below the sea, the ocean floor can be thrust upwards.
2. Marine animals such as snails and sea worms are displaced because the seafloor quickly becomes eroded.
3. People can prepare for a tsunami or hurricane if they are given advance warning.
4. ______________________________
____
5. ______________________________
____

Students write routinely for a range of tasks, purposes, and audiences. Students practice various conventions of standard English.

Name ______________________________

Reference Materials

DIRECTIONS Circle the part of speech of the underlined word in each sentence and write a definition. Then use a dictionary to clarify the part of speech and definition for each word. Revise the definitions to make them precise.

Part of Speech

1. This story is not futuristic because it takes place in the present. — **1.** noun verb

   Definition: ______________________

2. Our coach will present several awards at the sports banquet. — **2.** noun verb

   Definition: ______________________

3. We will reject applications that arrive after the deadline. — **3.** noun verb

   Definition: ______________________

4. The worker inspected each product and placed the rejects in the trash. — **4.** noun verb

   Definition: ______________________

5. Security will not permit you to go backstage without a pass. — **5.** noun verb

   Definition: ______________________

6. Do you have the proper permit to operate this boat? — **6.** noun verb

   Definition: ______________________

7. The company had a recall on several car models with faulty brakes. — **7.** noun verb

   Definition: ______________________

   ____

8. She did not recall why she had gone downstairs. — **8.** noun verb

   Definition: ______________________

Students apply grade-level word analysis skills.

Name ______________________________

Benchmark Vocabulary

DIRECTIONS Write a sentence using each word.

generating conservation renewable

____

____

____

____

____

____

Write in Response to Reading

The authors of "Offshore Wind Still the Best Bet for Clean Energy" and *Science Fair Showdown!* both think people should use renewable energy sources. Which text is more convincing? Use details from the text to support your answer. Write your paragraph below, on a separate sheet of paper, or in a new document.

____

____

____

____

____

____

____

____

____

____

Students demonstrate contextual understanding of Benchmark Vocabulary. Students read text closely and use text evidence in their written answers.

Name ______________________________

Evaluate Information Presented in Multiple Texts

DIRECTIONS Using evidence from the text, answer the following questions about "Offshore Wind Still the Best Bet for Clean Energy" and *Science Fair Showdown!*

1. According to the texts, why must we reduce our use of fossil fuels?

2. According to the article "Offshore Wind Still Best Bet for Clean Energy," what are ways to reduce greenhouse gas emissions?

3. Which energy sources do both texts address? Which text gives the most information about these sources?

4. "Offshore Wind Still the Best Bet for Clean Energy" states that most greenhouse gas emissions come from electricity generation, transportation, and heating buildings. What solutions might Sofia, Diya, and Albert offer to reduce greenhouse gas emissions?

Students analyze and respond to literary and informational text.

Name ______________________________

Writing

Argument Writing: Edit and Proofread a Persuasive Speech Reread your persuasive speech draft. Edit your draft to make sure you have followed the order of points in your outline and expressed your ideas clearly. Then proofread your draft to correct any errors in grammar and spelling. Make sure your final draft has the following:

- correct subject-verb agreement
- correct use of prepositions and conjunctions
- well-constructed dependent and independent clauses
- accurate use of domain-specific words
- correct, standard English spellings of all words

Write your revised speech on a separate sheet of paper or start a new document.

Conventions

Correct Run-On Sentences

DIRECTIONS Correct the run-on sentences below by rewriting them in the space provided.

1. Our apartment building now has a green roof this is making a difference to the air quality.

____

____

2. We thought it would be a difficult process actually the work progressed quickly.

____

____

3. The building residents were satisfied the construction company was experienced and professional.

____

____

Students write routinely for a range of tasks, purposes, and audiences. Students practice various conventions of standard English.

Name ______________________________

Benchmark Vocabulary

DIRECTIONS Write a sentence using each word.

severe expanding critical

____

____

____

____

____

____

Write in Response to Reading

Examine the visual features on page 25 of *Ocean Storm Alert!* and on pages 16–17 of *Science Fair Showdown!* Write a paragraph that compares and contrasts how these two visuals convey the authors' purpose and perspective in the texts. Use details from the texts to support your answer. Write your paragraph below, on a separate sheet of paper, or in a new document.

____

____

____

____

____

____

____

____

____

____

Students demonstrate contextual understanding of Benchmark Vocabulary. Students read text closely and use text evidence in their written answers.

Name ______________________________

Writing

Argument Writing: Publish and Present a Persuasive Speech Make a clean copy of your speech, checking that words are spelled correctly and errors have been fixed and removed from the document. Next, practice giving your speech in front of a mirror or with a partner. Remember to underline or highlight key points to emphasize during your presentation.
Write your final draft on a separate sheet of paper or start a new document.

Conventions

Spell Correctly

DIRECTIONS Add *-s* or *-es* to one word in each sentence below to spell plural nouns correctly and to show correct subject-verb agreement. In some words you will need to change *y* to *i* before adding *-es*. Rewrite the sentences on the lines provided.

1. The cloud are dark and heavy with rain.

____

____

2. A cloud carrys moisture until it becomes too full.

____

____

3. The dirty dish need to be washed right away!

____

____

4. Lee throw his pennys into the fountain to make his wishes.

____

____

5. She unwrap her gifts quickly on her birthday.

____

Students write routinely for a range of tasks, purposes, and audiences. Students practice various conventions of standard English.

Name ______________________________________

Benchmark Vocabulary

DIRECTIONS Write a sentence using each word.

consulted undertake expedition

____

____

____

____

____

____

Write in Response to Reading

Reread the third full paragraph on page 3 of *Journey to the Center of the Earth,* beginning with the word "Nevertheless." In this paragraph and the two that follow it, Axel describes his uncle as "a man of deep learning." Which text descriptions provide support for this analysis? Write your answer below, on a separate sheet of paper, or in a new document.

____

____

____

____

____

____

Students demonstrate contextual understanding of Benchmark Vocabulary. Students read text closely and use text evidence in their written answers.

Name ______________________________

Writing

Narrative Writing: Establish Setting Reread the indoor and outdoor setting descriptions on pages 1 and 6 of *Journey to the Center of the Earth.* Then write a description of a fantasy world that establishes a context for a fantasy narrative. Consider the following before writing:

- In what time period does the narrative take place?
- Where does the narrative take place?
- What sensory details can I add to make the setting come to life?

Use a separate sheet of paper or start a new document.

Conventions

Relative Pronouns

DIRECTIONS Complete the sentences below by filling in the blank with the correct relative pronoun.

1. The bird ____________ was injured landed on the sidewalk.
2. The boy ____________ plays the tuba in the school band is Jeremy.
3. The receipt, ____________ was for the shirt I just bought, must have slipped out of my purse.
4. The dog ____________ hid under the bed was afraid of lightning.
5. The little girl ____________ rides her bike every day always wears a helmet.

Students write routinely for a range of tasks, purposes, and audiences. Students practice various conventions of standard English.

Name ____________________

Figurative Language

DIRECTIONS For each item, underline the example of figurative language, write the type of figurative language (metaphor or simile), and write its meaning.

1. Gary left a maze of instructions on how to care for his pet ferret.

Type: ____________________

Meaning: ____________________

2. When she saw the destruction caused by the fire, Holly cried a river of tears.

Type: ____________________

Meaning: ____________________

3. During practice, our coach is as demanding as a drill sergeant.

Type: ____________________

Meaning: ____________________

4. The puppy cried like an unoiled hinge until he got a dog treat.

Type: ____________________

Meaning: ____________________

5. Jane was the mother hen of the group, making sure everyone ate a good breakfast.

Type: ____________________

Meaning: ____________________

Students apply grade-level word analysis skills.

Name ______________________________

Benchmark Vocabulary

DIRECTIONS Write a sentence using each word.

attain ascend interior

____

____

____

____

____

____

Write in Response to Reading

Reread pages 37–38 of *Journey to the Center of the Earth.* On these pages, Grauben explains her position about the journey to Axel. What does she tell him? How do her words conflict with Axel's thoughts about the journey? Write your answer below, on a separate sheet of paper, or in a new document.

____

____

____

____

____

____

____

____

____

____

____

Students demonstrate contextual understanding of Benchmark Vocabulary. Students read text closely and use text evidence in their written answers.

Name ____________________

Analyze Conflict

DIRECTIONS Use evidence from the text to answer the following questions about *Journey to the Center of the Earth.*

1. Reread the text on page 28. What does the reader learn about Axel's inner conflict about taking the journey with his uncle?

2. On page 29, how does the relationship between Axel and Liedenbrock change, and what new conflict results from this?

3. On page 33, why does Axel claim that he is no longer interested in discussing his uncle's speculation about the journey? How does Liedenbrock reply?

4. On pages 36–37, what is Axel's inner conflict after his meeting with Liedenbrock? How does he feel? What does he say and do?

Students analyze and respond to literary and informational text.

Name ______________________________

Narrative Writing: Develop Multiple Characters Reread pages 20–22 in *Journey to the Center of the Earth* and think about how the relationship between Professor Liedenbrock and Axel affects the plot of the narrative. Then write several paragraphs describing the two most important characters in your fantasy narrative. Make sure you describe the conflict between these two characters and how that conflict drives the plot. Consider the following before writing: Use a separate sheet of paper or start a new document.

- What does each character look like?
- How should I describe each character's personality?
- What events in each character's past have an impact on his or her actions in the narrative?

____

____

____

____

Use Intensive Pronouns

DIRECTIONS Complete the sentences below by circling the correct intensive pronoun.

1. I (myself / herself) sailed the boat into the harbor.
2. Luis (themselves / himself) solved the difficult puzzle without help from his family.
3. The bees (themselves / yourselves) are the ones that made the honey.
4. We (yourselves / ourselves) found the buried treasure by following the map.
5. You (yourself / themselves) can change the world with one small act of kindness.

Students write routinely for a range of tasks, purposes, and audiences. Students practice various conventions of standard English.

Name ______________________________

Benchmark Vocabulary

DIRECTIONS Write a sentence using each word.

terminating   inhabitant   provisions

____
____
____
____
____
____

Write in Response to Reading

Reread page 56 of *Journey to the Center of the Earth.* What is the purpose of the conversation between Fridrikssen and Liedenbrock about the library and the books? Explain how this helps to advance the plot.

____
____
____
____
____
____
____

Students demonstrate contextual understanding of Benchmark Vocabulary. Students read text closely and use text evidence in their written answers.

Name ______________________________ **Sleuth Passage**

Surviving Against Odds

Throughout history, people have learned to survive in harsh conditions. The Bedouin (BED oo in) live in deserts of the Middle East and North Africa, some of the most inhospitable places in the word. They know from experience how to find fresh water in the dew on desert grass or under stones in the sand. For centuries, before the use of maps and compasses, the Bedouin followed tracks during the day and the North Star at night to find their way—often on camels—in the vast expanses of sand.

Far from the desert regions where the Bedouin live, modern outdoor adventurers can take courses in desert survival techniques. Trained survivalists or park rangers lead these hands-on programs. Most participants quickly recognize lack of water and extreme temperatures as the two main dangers. Instructors advise them how to find shade or build shelter to survive in high temperatures (up to 120°F). To obtain water, leaders demonstrate how to seal a plastic bag over a green plant. The plant's leaves produce moisture that then collects in the bag. As a last resort, crushing a cactus can produce enough water to quench one's thirst temporarily. Students learn how to prevent heat stroke during the day and ways to stay warm at night. They and their instructors watch out for desert hazards like poisonous plants, snakes, lizards, and scorpions.

Participants know that the course will end soon and they aren't really stranded. But why would anyone choose such a rigorous excursion? Perhaps these outdoor enthusiasts enjoy living close to nature, or maybe they thrive on extreme physical and mental challenges. It is also possible they feel the experience will prepare them for the unexpected.

If you hike or routinely ride through large stretches of desert, keep in mind a few simple tips. First, carry a survival kit with basic supplies such as matches, sunscreen, a knife, a container to hold water, a compass, and a mirror to use for signaling. Second, conserve your energy and plan to travel at night when temperatures fall. Third, ration your water. Take small sips frequently. Finally, dress appropriately! You might think you'll be cooler if you take off layers of clothing when you're sweating, but clothing actually helps your body cool down. It prevents sweat from evaporating too quickly. Also, clothing will help protect you from sunburn. If you follow these tips, you should be able to stay safe and survive in the desert.

Students read text closely to determine what the text says.

Name ______________________________

Gather Evidence Reread the first two paragraphs of the text. What words or phrases does the author use to describe the desert environment? Circle the words in the text.

Gather Evidence: Extend Your Ideas How do these words help you understand what a traveler needs to take on a trip to the desert?

____

____

____

Ask Questions Write one question you might ask the program instructor of a desert survival class. Include a detail from the text in your question.

____

____

Ask Questions: Extend Your Ideas Now pretend you are the program instructor. Use evidence from the text to answer the question you asked.

____

____

____

Make Your Case Underline items in the text that might be included in a survival kit. Then write a sentence telling why someone might need one of these items in a desert.

____

____

Make Your Case: Extend Your Ideas How would a survival kit help a traveler in the desert?

____

____

____

Students read text closely to determine what the text says.

Name ______________________________

Writing

Narrative Writing: Establish Point of View Reread pages 46–47 of *Journey to the Center of the Earth* and think about the impact of first-person point of view on the story. Then write a one- to two-page introduction that establishes the fantasy world in your story. Before writing, ask yourself:

- Do I want one of the characters to tell the story?
- Do I want an outside narrator to tell the story?
- If I choose a narrator to tell the story, which of the characters' thoughts and feelings will the narrator know?

Write your introduction on a separate sheet of paper or start a new document.

Conventions

Recognize and Correct Vague Pronouns

DIRECTIONS Revise the sentences below by correcting the vague pronouns.

1. They marched in time during the band's halftime show.

____

____

2. The rooster's crowing woke him up, so the farmer got out of bed.

____

____

3. It turns red when it is ripe. Jenna will pick the strawberry.

____

____

4. They said I needed to sweep and dust the house before I could go out.

____

____

Students write routinely for a range of tasks, purposes, and audiences. Students practice various conventions of standard English.

Name ____________________

Benchmark Vocabulary

DIRECTIONS Write a sentence using each word.

persistency elevation stupefied

Write in Response to Reading

Reread pages 71–72 of *Journey to the Center of the Earth.* How does the author describe the travelers' hosts? What words are used, and how do they help the reader to understand Axel's character? Write your answer below, on a separate sheet of paper, or in a new document.

Students demonstrate contextual understanding of Benchmark Vocabulary. Students read text closely and use text evidence in their written answers.

Name ______________________________

Analyze Language

DIRECTIONS Using evidence from the text, answer the following questions about *Journey to the Center of the Earth.*

1. Look at the second to last paragraph on page 69, where Liedenbrock is battling with his horse. What words does the author use for describing Liedenbrock after this battle, and what does this suggest about the battle's outcome?

____

____

____

2. Contrast the first two homes where the travelers stayed (pages 71, 77–78). What words does the author use for describing the hospitality of these homes?

____

____

____

3. On page 90, what words does the author use for describing Axel's reaction to the discovery of the script on the wall? What does this tell the reader about Axel?

____

____

____

____

4. On pages 90–91, how does the author describe Liedenbrock as he waits for the sun to appear? What words does he use, and what does this tell the reader about Liedenbrock?

____

____

____

____

Students analyze and respond to literary and informational text.

Name ______________________

Writing

Narrative Writing: Establish Conflict and Plot Sequence Reread pages 79–81 in *Journey to the Center of the Earth.* Think about how the conflict between Axel and Professor Liedenbrock has advanced the story up to this point, and how the writer moves from realistic events to fantastical events. Then create a sequence of events that includes:

- the main conflict between the opposing characters.
- the resolution to the conflict.
- the climax of the story.
- the important events that lead up to the climax.

Write your plot sequence on a separate sheet of paper or start a new document.

Conventions

Recognize and Correct Vague Pronouns

DIRECTIONS Revise the sentences below by correcting the vague or incorrect pronouns.

1. Rodney and Leah walked into room 124 for her math class.

____

2. When Jacob rode his bike to Andrew's house, he fell.

____

3. Luz went to the library and checked it out.

____

4. I have a new sweater and jeans. I got it for my birthday.

____

5. Dora told her sister a story and she was scared.

____

Students write routinely for a range of tasks, purposes, and audiences. Students practice various conventions of standard English.

Name ______________________________

Benchmark Vocabulary

DIRECTIONS Write a sentence using each word.

transition splendor

____

____

____

____

Write in Response to Reading

Reread page 124 of *Journey to the Center of the Earth,* where Axel and Professor Liedenbrock agree to let the water run free. What can you infer about the characters from this dialogue? Write your answer below, on a separate sheet of paper, or in a new document.

____

____

____

____

____

____

____

____

____

____

____

____

____

Students demonstrate contextual understanding of Benchmark Vocabulary. Students read text closely and use text evidence in their written answers.

Name ______________________________

Writing

Narrative Writing: Use Dialogue and Description Reread pages 104–106 and 112–113 of *Journey to the Center of the Earth.* Notice how dialogue and description are used to advance the plot of the story. Then write three or more pages to develop the rising action that will lead to the climax of your story. Write your rising action on a separate sheet of paper or start a new document.

Conventions

Use Commas in a Series

DIRECTIONS Rewrite the sentences by adding commas in the correct places.

1. Amy Peter Luis and Maya got the highest grades on the science test.

____

____

2. At the mall, Linda bought a shirt Dan bought a wallet and Steve bought some socks.

____

____

3. Michelle couldn't decide if she should ride her bike go for a walk or swim in the pool.

____

____

4. Mom's hobbies are reading jogging gardening and knitting.

____

5. Lana does not like cooking shopping or cleaning.

____

Students write routinely for a range of tasks, purposes, and audiences. Students practice various conventions of standard English.

Name ____________________

Benchmark Vocabulary

DIRECTIONS Write a sentence using each word.

perilous destination anguish

Write in Response to Reading

Reread page 125 of *Journey to the Center of the Earth.* How has Axel's view of the mission changed, and how does he explain this change? Be sure to include evidence that supports your answers. Write your answer below, on a separate sheet of paper, or in a new document.

Students demonstrate contextual understanding of Benchmark Vocabulary. Students read text closely and use text evidence in their written answers.

Name ____________________

Writing

Narrative Writing: Establish Pace of Events Reread pages 139–146 of *Journey to the Center of the Earth.* Think about how the techniques such as adjusting sentence length and dialogue are used to set the pace of the story, and remember that the goal is to keep the reader engaged leading up to the climax of the narrative. Revise your own fantasy narrative, adjusting the pace as needed. Make sure that your revisions add to the reader's enjoyment of the story.

Write your revisions on a separate sheet of paper or start a new document.

Conventions

Semicolons in a Series

DIRECTIONS Add the commas and semicolons that are needed in each sentence.

1. I have book reports due on October 1 2016 November 12 2016 and December 8 2016.

2. Jeff enjoys eating eggs bacon and toast for breakfast soup pasta and pizza for lunch and chicken steak and vegetables for dinner.

3. Amanda has sweaters in red blue and yellow socks in purple black and green and pants in blue tan and black.

4. Marcus goes to jazz orchestra and pop concerts with his mom big band rock and marching band concerts with his dad and rock reggae and rap concerts with his cousins.

5. Mrs. Lambert graded math reading and writing homework on Monday science social studies and writing homework on Tuesday and math science and reading homework on Wednesday.

Students write routinely for a range of tasks, purposes, and audiences. Students practice various conventions of standard English.

Name ____________________

Analogies

DIRECTIONS Write the type of relationship that the first word pair in the analogy shows (cause/effect, part/whole, item/category). Then write the word from the Word Bank that best completes the analogy.

Word Bank

biology	destruction	tail	soil	stadium
condiment	mastery	bouquet	fuel	profession

		Relationship
1.	stage : auditorium :: field : ____________	**1.** ____________
2.	poetry : literature :: ____________ : science	**2.** ____________
3.	wheat : grain :: mustard : ____________	**3.** ____________
4.	ignoring : neglect :: practice : ____________	**4.** ____________
5.	knitting : hobby :: doctor : ____________	**5.** ____________
6.	drought : famine :: earthquake : ____________	**6.** ____________
7.	wool : fiber :: diesel : ____________	**7.** ____________
8.	chapter : book :: ____________ : kite	**8.** ____________
9.	soccer : sport :: clay : ____________	**9.** ____________
10.	student : class :: flower : ____________	**10.** ____________

Students apply grade-level word analysis skills.

Name ______________________________

Benchmark Vocabulary

DIRECTIONS Write a sentence using each word.

inexplicable excavation invigorated

____

____

____

____

____

____

Write in Response to Reading

How does the dialogue between Axel and Professor Liedenbrock on p. 162 help to move the plot forward? Write your response below or on a separate sheet of paper.

____

____

____

____

____

____

____

____

____

____

____

____

Students analyze and respond to literary and informational text.

Name ______________________________ **Reading Analysis**

Analyze Plot Events

DIRECTIONS Using evidence from the text, answer the following questions about *Journey to the Center of the Earth.*

1. On page 150, Axel says, “Well, I am afraid my brain is affected.” What does he mean, and how does this give more information about the plot?

2. On page 151, how does Liedenbrock help prepare Axel for the next part of their voyage?

3. How are Hans’s actions useful for plot development on pages 161–162?

Students demonstrate contextual understanding of Benchmark Vocabulary. Students read text closely and use text evidence in their written answers.

Name ____________________

Writing

Narrative Writing: Use Language to Clarify and Engage Reread pages 153–154 of *Journey to the Center of the Earth* and think about how sensory details and figurative language are used to advance the plot of the story. Then revise your own fantasy narrative to add similar details. Make sure to add details that engage all of a reader's senses, and use figurative language that fits your characters in the story. Write your revisions on a separate sheet of paper or start a new document.

Conventions

Use Commas with Introductory Elements

DIRECTIONS Rewrite the sentences below, adding commas in the appropriate places.

1. Eventually I got around to finishing my chores.

____

2. In fact I finished my chores before going to Sam's house.

____

3. By the way Dad wants you to wash the dishes.

____

4. No Mom didn't say that you can wash the dishes tomorrow.

____

5. If I were you I would do my chores today.

____

Students write routinely for a range of tasks, purposes, and audiences. Students practice various conventions of standard English.

Name ______________________________

Benchmark Vocabulary

DIRECTIONS Write a sentence using each word.

skeptically aggravated

____

____

____

____

____

____

Write in Response to Reading

On page 165, Axel's notes reflect that they see nothing on the horizon, and on page 166, Axel begins dreaming. What is the author's purpose in sharing these events with the reader? Write your answer below, on a separate sheet of paper, or in a new document.

____

____

____

____

____

____

____

____

____

____

____

Students demonstrate contextual understanding of Benchmark Vocabulary. Students read text closely and use text evidence in their written answers.

Name ______________________________

Author's Purpose

DIRECTIONS Using evidence from the text, answer the following questions about *Journey to the Center of the Earth.*

1. On pages 163–164, Axel suggests naming a port after Grauben, his love interest, and his uncle agrees to this. Why does the author include this event in the story?

2. On pages 165–166, Axel and the Professor examine an unusual fish that Hans has caught. What is the author's purpose in describing this unusual fish to the reader?

3. On pages 169–170, Axel remarks that Liedenbrock appears to be anxious, which in turn leads to dialogue that has been absent for a long part of their journey. What is the author's purpose in describing this dialogue to the reader?

Students analyze and respond to literary and informational text.

Name ____________________

Writing

Narrative Writing: Use Transitions to Convey Sequence Revise your fantasy narrative using transition words, phrases, and clauses. Make sure your transitions add to the reader's understanding of the story. Write your revisions on a separate sheet of paper or start a new document.

Conventions

Use Commas with *Yes* and *No*

DIRECTIONS Rewrite the sentences and add commas in the appropriate places.

1. Yes I have seen that movie before.

____

2. No my sister is not tall enough to ride the new roller coaster.

____

3. No I have not found my blue sweater yet.

____

4. Yes I got a good grade on my math test.

____

5. Yes Laurie is my best friend.

____

6. No Jim is not ready for school yet.

____

Students write routinely for a range of tasks, purposes, and audiences. Students practice various conventions of standard English.

Name ____________________

Benchmark Vocabulary

DIRECTIONS Write a sentence using each word.

eccentricities elapsed

Write in Response to Reading

Reread page 210 of *Journey to the Center of the Earth.* How does the discovery of a blocked hole lead the story to its climax? Write your answer below, on a separate sheet of paper, or in a new document.

Students demonstrate contextual understanding of Benchmark Vocabulary. Students read text closely and use text evidence in their written answers.

Name ______________________

Writing

Narrative Writing: Write a Conclusion Write a conclusion for your own fantasy story that shows:

- how the characters have changed based on the lessons they have learned.
- how the protagonist resolves the conflict.
- what lessons the protagonist has learned from their experiences.

Write your revisions on a separate sheet of paper or start a new document.

Conventions

Use Commas with Tag Questions

DIRECTIONS Rewrite the sentences adding a tag question to each sentence. Make sure you use commas correctly.

1. You don't need to go to the store.

____

2. We have math homework today.

____

3. You like apples.

____

4. He shouldn't drive so fast.

____

5. We should learn to speak Spanish.

____

6. Marie couldn't finish her homework.

____

Students write routinely for a range of tasks, purposes, and audiences. Students practice various conventions of standard English.

Benchmark Vocabulary

Name ______________________________

DIRECTIONS Write a sentence using each word.

multitude perish

____

____

____

____

Write in Response to Reading

On page 238, Hans leaves for Iceland. Why is this event significant to the plot's resolution? Write your answer on the lines below, on a separate sheet of paper, or in a new document.

____

____

____

____

____

____

____

____

____

____

____

____

____

Students demonstrate contextual understanding of Benchmark Vocabulary. Students read text closely and use text evidence in their written answers.

Name ____________________

Analyze Plot Resolution

DIRECTIONS Using evidence from the text, answer the following questions about *Journey to the Center of the Earth.*

1. On page 216, Axel determines that they have very little food left. Why is this important for the falling action of the story?

____
____
____
____

2. On page 220, after Axel questions Liedenbrock about ways that they might die, the Professor shrugs his shoulders. How does this relate to the falling action of the story?

____
____
____
____
____

3. How are Axel and Professor Liedenbrock's lives changed as a result of their journey? Provide evidence from the text to support your answer.

____
____
____
____
____
____
____

Students analyze and respond to literary and informational text.

Name ______________________________

Writing

Narrative Writing: Draw Evidence from Literary Texts to Support Analysis
Reread pages 224–239 of *Journey to the Center of the* Earth and think about how the author created a world beneath the Earth. Write an analysis of the narrative elements of the story. Make sure to include the following elements:

- Setting: the physical location where the story takes place
- Characters: their personalities, behaviors, actions, and relationships with others
- Plot: how the events impact the climax or resolution
- Theme: determine the main idea behind the story

Write your analysis on a separate sheet of paper or start a new document.

Conventions

Use Commas to Indicate Direct Address

DIRECTIONS Revise the sentences by adding commas to indicate direct address, as needed.

1. Is that your guitar Sammy or is it Eddie's?
2. Tell me how to play your favorite song Jessica.
3. How old were you when you learned to play the banjo Lester?
4. Sheila would you like to play drums or piano?
5. Can you be in charge of the metronome Nate until Mr. Duncan returns?
6. Eden it is your turn to play bass guitar.

Students write routinely for a range of tasks, purposes, and audiences. Students practice various conventions of standard English.

Name ______________________________

Benchmark Vocabulary

DIRECTIONS Write a sentence using each word.

tirade sinister expel

____

____

____

____

____

____

Write in Response to Reading

DIRECTIONS Reread pages 144–146 of *The Monster in the Mountain*. Write a paragraph describing the fantasy world of Animos. Use details from the text to support your answer. Write your answer below, on a separate sheet of paper, or in a new document.

____

____

____

____

____

____

____

____

____

____

____

Students demonstrate contextual understanding of Benchmark Vocabulary. Students read text closely and use text evidence in their written answers.

Name ____________________

Writing

Narrative Writing: Balance Elements of Reality and Fantasy Write a short science fiction or fantasy story. Remember to select a real event from your own life to use as a basis for your story.

Write your story on a separate sheet of paper or start a new document.

Conventions

Underline Titles of Works

DIRECTIONS Revise the sentences by underlining text to show titles of creative works.

1. Would you like to see the movie The Martian with me on Friday?
2. The band Journey released their album Escape in July of 1981.
3. Have you read To Kill a Mockingbird by Harper Lee?
4. Did you know that The Fault in Our Stars by John Green was made into a movie?
5. My family looks forward to seeing a local production of The Nutcracker every winter.
6. Tales of a Fourth Grade Nothing by Judy Blume is one of the first chapter books I ever read.

Students write routinely for a range of tasks, purposes, and audiences. Students practice various conventions of standard English.

Name ______________________________

Connotation and Denotation

DIRECTIONS Replace the underlined word in each sentence with a word from the Word Bank that has a similar denotation but a positive connotation.

Word Bank

absorbed	remarkable	firm	inexpensive	variable
slim	restless	trusting	chatty	confident

1. I found a strange purple rock on my walk through the woods. 1. ______________
2. The young man who walked into the classroom had long legs and a skinny build. 2. ______________
3. I bought three pairs of pants at the sale because they were so cheap. 3. ______________
4. The runner challenges anyone to beat her time because she is arrogant. 4. ______________
5. She is so obsessed that she spends all of her free time in her art studio. 5. ______________
6. The child was too fidgety to sit through the orchestra recital. 6. ______________
7. She was gullible and did not know what she was getting into. 7. ______________
8. The theater has some very strict rules that we must follow. 8. ______________
9. The weather along the coast can be erratic. 9. ______________
10. My aunt is very gossipy when she comes to visit. 10. ______________

Students apply grade-level word analysis skills.

Name ______________________________

Benchmark Vocabulary

DIRECTIONS Write a sentence using each word.

immense ominous colossal

____

____

____

____

____

____

Write in Response to Reading

Reread pages 42–50 of *Journey to the Center of the Earth* and pages 140–144 in *The Monster in the Mountain*. Write a paragraph comparing and contrasting how the explorers in *Journey to the Center of the Earth* traveled to Rejkiavik with how the characters in *The Monster in the Mountain* arrive in the realm of Animos. Explain what is realistic and what is impossible. Write your answer below, on a separate sheet of paper, or in a new document.

____

____

____

____

____

____

____

____

____

____

Students demonstrate contextual understanding of Benchmark Vocabulary. Students read text closely and use text evidence in their written answers.

Name ____________________

Compare and Contrast Genres

DIRECTIONS Using evidence from the text, answer the following questions about *Journey to the Center of the Earth* and *The Monster in the Mountain*.

1. On page 153 in *Journey to the Center of the Earth*, the author describes a vast sea. How might this passage differ if it were part of a fantasy text?

2. On pages 144–145 in *The Monster in the Mountain,* the author describes the teens' first glimpse of Animos. How might this description differ if it were part of a science fiction text?

3. On pages 236–239 in *Journey to the Center of the Earth* and pages 161–163 in *The Monster in the Mountain*, the texts reach a resolution. How do these resolutions reflect the different themes of the texts?

Students analyze and respond to literary and informational text.

Writing

Name ______________________________

Narrative Writing: Research a Topic Think about the scientific subjects that are mentioned in *Journey to the Center of the Earth* and *The Monster in the Mountain*. Writers use real facts in order to make their stories seem reasonable. Now you will be writing your own science fiction story, including a main character who is a weather expert. In order to write this story, research the weather and its effects. Write your research on a separate sheet of paper or start a new document.

Conventions

Use Italics for Titles of Works

DIRECTIONS Circle the titles of creative works that should appear in italics within each sentence.

1. The Wizard of Oz is a popular book that was made into a movie.
2. My favorite actor starred in the movie version of Oliver.
3. Who has read My Side of the Mountain by Jean Craighead George?
4. I could read the novel The Call of the Wild over and over again.
5. The author spoke about writing My Summer in Mexico.
6. The Adventures of Jesse is one of my favorite trilogies.

Students write routinely for a range of tasks, purposes, and audiences. Students practice various conventions of standard English.

Name ______________________________

Benchmark Vocabulary

DIRECTIONS Write a sentence using each word.

stiflingly jolted profusely

____

____

____

____

____

____

Write in Response to Reading

Reread page 165 of *Galveston Journal: September 1900*. Why do you think Delia was so excited about her birthday gift? Use details from the text to support your answer. Write your answer below, on a separate sheet of paper, or in a new document.

____

____

____

____

____

____

____

____

____

____

____

Students demonstrate contextual understanding of Benchmark Vocabulary. Students read text closely and use text evidence in their written answers.

Name ____________________

Underwater Explorer

By the middle of the twentieth century, it seemed that almost the entire world had been explored. Adventurers had visited Mount Everest, the South Pole, and the North Pole, along with the densest forests and the driest deserts Earth had to offer. It was not a great time for a person to try to make a name for himself as an explorer. But Jacques-Yves Cousteau (coo STOH) was not daunted by the fact that almost every spot on dry land had already been visited by someone. Instead, Cousteau made a name for himself by exploring what many considered the last frontier of Earth—the oceans.

Born in 1910 in France, Cousteau began his studies of the oceans around 1936. Over the next few years, he did a considerable amount of deep-sea diving; in 1943, he dove about 59 feet (18 meters) into the ocean and made a short film about what the world looked like that far underwater. A few years later, Cousteau helped develop better and more reliable gear for underwater travel, making it possible for adventurers—such as Cousteau himself—to spend more and more time underwater. Between the 1950s and the 1970s, Cousteau carried out a number of studies involving the oceans and marine life. For example, he located shipwrecks and studied them closely. He also made some important discoveries regarding porpoises and their use of sonar to navigate. In addition, he spread a message of environmental awareness by encouraging people not to pollute the oceans.

Cousteau developed a variety of machines and vehicles that could travel deeper into the ocean. In 1956, for instance, he built a saucerlike vehicle that could reach 1,148 feet (350 meters) into the sea. A decade later he designed another one that traveled 1,640 feet (500 meters) below the surface. Throughout his time underwater, Cousteau filmed the undersea world and later shared the films with people across the world. His work greatly increased knowledge of the oceans and its lifeforms.

Through this work Cousteau became famous—and somewhat controversial. Several scientists charged that he was too interested in popularizing the world below the ocean surface and not interested enough in studying it. Today some claim also that because Cousteau was not a trained oceanographer—a scientist who studies the ocean— he sometimes oversimplified scientific ideas in his books, films, and lectures. Despite this controversy, Cousteau remains well-known today for his work. Cousteau died in 1997 after a long and adventure-filled life.

Students read text closely to determine what the text says.

Name ____

Sleuth Work

Gather Evidence Underline the inventions Cousteau made to explore the ocean.

Gather Evidence: Extend Your Ideas Why do you think Cousteau wanted to go deeper into the ocean?

____

____

____

Ask Questions Circle the section in the text about Cousteau's message of environmental awareness. Then brainstorm one question you have about this message.

____

____

____

Ask Questions: Extend Your Ideas How would you go about finding the answer to your question?

____

____

____

Make Your Case What sentences from the text provide evidence of the author's opinion about Jacques Cousteau?

____

____

____

____

Students read text closely to determine what the text says.

Name ______________________________

Narrative Writing: Plan/Prewrite Continue working on your science fiction story by planning and prewriting for the story. Make sure you incorporate information from your research. In this planning stage, you should create a story map that includes the conflict between two characters, the rising action, the climax, and the resolution. Also include detailed descriptions of the main characters and setting. Write your story map on a separate sheet of paper or start a new document.

Use Quotation Marks for Titles of Works

DIRECTIONS Add quotation marks to the titles of creative works in each sentence.

1. Falling Leaves is one of my favorite poems.
2. My little sister just turned three, and she wants me to sing Happy Birthday to her every day.
3. They play The Star-Spangled Banner before every major sporting event.
4. I enjoyed reading the chapter A Barren Land in *Journey to the Center of the Earth.*
5. Dreamtime is the title of a song by my favorite artist.
6. Stopping by Woods on a Snowy Evening by Robert Frost is a great poem to read during a snowstorm.

Students write routinely for a range of tasks, purposes, and audiences. Students practice various conventions of standard English.

Name ______

Benchmark Vocabulary

DIRECTIONS Write a sentence using each word.

raging collapsed grisly

______

Write in Response to Reading

Reread pages 187 and 190 of *Galveston Journal: September 1900*. Why do you think that Delia clutches her silver pendant? Use details from the text to support your answer. Write your answer below, on a separate sheet of paper, or in a new document.

______

Students demonstrate contextual understanding of Benchmark Vocabulary. Students read text closely and use text evidence in their written answers.

Name ______________________________

Analyze Cause and Effect

DIRECTIONS Using evidence from the text, answer the following questions about pages 176–184 of *Galveston Journal: September 1900*.

1. On what day did the storm strike? What caused Delia to wait for days before writing about the storm?

____

____

____

____

2. What was the cause of Mr. Johnson's weeping on page 181? In contrast, what caused Delia to stay dry-eyed?

____

____

____

____

3. How was the rest of the country able to learn about the storm that damaged Galveston? What effect does this have on Galveston?

____

____

____

____

Students analyze and respond to literary and informational text.

Name ______________________________

Writing

Narrative Writing: Draft a Science Fiction Story Continue working on your own science fiction story by writing a first draft of your story. Use the research about weather that you completed in the previous lessons. Be sure to use your story map as your guide for writing. Remember the following as you write:

- The events in the rising action should lead to the story's climax.
- Using dialogue can help advance the plot and speed up the pace of the action.
- Science fiction is rooted in scientific facts, so make sure you incorporate your research.
- One of the main characters of the story must be an expert on the weather.
- Use transition words and phrases to move smoothly from one scene to the next.

Write your draft on a separate sheet of paper or start a new document.

Conventions

Use Commas to Set Off Nonrestrictive/Parenthetical Elements

DIRECTIONS Add commas to each sentence that has nonrestrictive elements. If there are no commas needed, leave the sentence as is.

1. My math test which had twenty questions was really challenging.

____

____

2. The dog which is white with black spots got adopted yesterday.

____

____

3. The firefighter who lives next door checked smoke detectors for everyone in the neighborhood.

____

4. The book which was written fifty years ago is still a favorite among children.

____

____

Students write routinely for a range of tasks, purposes, and audiences. Students practice various conventions of standard English.

Name ______________________________

Benchmark Vocabulary

DIRECTIONS Write a sentence using each word.

intense obstacle despair

____

____

____

____

____

____

Write in Response to Reading

Reread page 229 of *Journey to the Center of the Earth* and pages 176–181 of *Galveston Journal: September 1900*. What heroic qualities of Hans and Mr. Johnson can you infer from text evidence? Use details from the text to support your answer. Write your answer below, on a separate sheet of paper, or in a new document.

____

____

____

____

____

____

____

____

____

____

Students demonstrate contextual understanding of Benchmark Vocabulary. Students read text closely and use text evidence in their written answers.

Name ______________________________

Writing

Narrative Writing: Review and Revise Science Fiction Continue working on your own science fiction story by reviewing and making revisions to your story. You can have your peers review your draft and then make revisions based on those reviews. Here are some tips for completing peer reviews:

- Give suggestions for improving the important events in the story.
- Point out any parts of the story that are confusing or unclear.
- Give suggestions for adjustments to pacing and transitions.
- Point out what you like about the story.

Write your revisions on a separate sheet of paper or start a new document.

Conventions

Use Parentheses to Set Off Nonrestrictive/Parenthetical Elements

DIRECTIONS Add parentheses to each sentence around the nonrestrictive elements.

1. Jon and Devon who are friends won the doubles tennis match.

   ____

   ____

2. Libby my cousin is a straight-A student.

   ____

3. Krista the flute player has four older brothers.

   ____

4. The coffee maker which Mom bought online is broken.

   ____

5. The apple which was green fell out of the basket.

   ____

Students write routinely for a range of tasks, purposes, and audiences. Students practice various conventions of standard English.

Name ____________________

Benchmark Vocabulary

DIRECTIONS Write a sentence using each word.

a-blowing different

____

____

____

____

Write in Response to Reading

Reread the "The Wind" on page 203. How does the author use comparison within the poem? What is the impact of this poetic device on the meaning and tone of the poem? Use details from the text to support your answer. Write your answer below, on a separate sheet of paper, or in a new document.

____

____

____

____

____

____

____

____

____

____

____

____

Students demonstrate contextual understanding of Benchmark Vocabulary. Students read text closely and use text evidence in their written answers.

Name ______________________________

Writing

Narrative Writing: Edit Continue working on your science fiction story by editing your story. Since it can be difficult to find errors in your own story, you should also have a classmate read your story and point out any errors that he or she may find. Write your revisions on a separate sheet of paper or start a new document.

Conventions

Use Dashes to Set Off Nonrestrictive/Parenthetical Elements

DIRECTIONS Rewrite each sentence and add dashes around the nonrestrictive/ parenthetical elements.

1. When the blizzard ended and ten inches of snow were on the ground we shoveled the driveway.

____

____

2. Jake and I went to a concert it was fun on Friday night.

____

____

3. My cousins Marc and Lesean go to my school.

____

____

4. April's dog a golden retriever ran away.

____

____

5. Mom used the bananas brown and mushy ones to make banana bread.

____

____

Students write routinely for a range of tasks, purposes, and audiences. Students practice various conventions of standard English.

Name ______________________________

Greek and Latin Suffixes *-logy, -ician, -crat, -ory*

DIRECTIONS Write the word from the Word Bank that has the same meaning as and can replace the words inside the brackets in each sentence. Use a print or digital dictionary as needed.

WORD BANK

anthropologist	astrology	cardiology	mathematician	preparatory
predatory	neurologist	clinician	autocrat	expository

1. The (doctor who specializes in nerve diseases) did a study on lack of sleep.

   ____

2. Both lawyers need to do (relating to preparation for a task) work before the trial.

   ____

3. When I need help with geometry, I ask my uncle, the (specialist in math).

   ____

4. I wrote a(n) (intended to explain or describe) article for my final paper.

   ____

5. I want to know how the heart functions, so I am studying (science of the heart).

   ____

6. The (ruler who has absolute power) had to flee the country and live in exile in France.

   ____

7. Dr. Frye is a great (doctor who works directly with patients) who always listens.

   ____

8. The (person who studies human cultures) is interested in families in ancient China.

   ____

9. A hawk is one example of a(n) (relating to an animal that hunts prey) animal.

   ____

10. Reading about (the study of how heavenly bodies influence people) is fun!

   ____

Students apply grade-level word analysis skills.

Name ______________________________

Benchmark Vocabulary

DIRECTIONS Write a sentence using each word.

hurling horrific

____

____

____

____

Write in Response to Reading

Reread page 165 of *Galveston Journal: September 1900* and page 203 of "The Wind." How are Delia and the speaker of the poem similar, and how are they different? Use details from the text to support your answer. Write your answer below, on a separate sheet of paper, or in a new document.

____

____

____

____

____

____

____

____

____

____

____

____

Students demonstrate contextual understanding of Benchmark Vocabulary. Students read text closely and use text evidence in their written answers.

Name ______________________________

Compare and Contrast Genres

DIRECTIONS Using evidence from the text, answer the following questions about *Galveston Journal: September 1900* and "The Wind."

1. The narrator and speaker in both texts experience the force of the wind firsthand. How do their experiences differ? How are they similar?

____

____

____

____

____

____

2. In what other way can these two genres be compared in their approach to the wind?

____

____

____

____

Students analyze and respond to literary and informational text.

Name ______________________________

Writing

Narrative Writing: Publish and Present a Science Fiction Story Publish and present your science fiction story by recording it as a radio play. You may wish to have classmates play different roles in your story. Consider adding sound effects to the recording. Write your radio play script on a separate sheet of paper or start a new document.

Conventions

Spell Correctly

DIRECTIONS Rewrite each sentence and correct all spelling errors.

1. Jane and Samantha went to the movies by themselfes.

2. The story ended with the elfs saving the little girles.

3. My dad built a bookcase with five shelfs.

4. We collected 500 seashells by ourselfs at the beach.

5. We cut the pizza slices into halfs to make them easier to eat.

Students write routinely for a range of tasks, purposes, and audiences. Students practice various conventions of standard English.

Name ____________________

Benchmark Vocabulary

DIRECTIONS Write a sentence using each word.

remarkable endure ferocious

Write in Response to Reading

Reread page 239 of *Journey to the Center of the Earth,* page 163 of *The Monster in the Mountain,* page 197 of *Galveston Journal: September 1900,* and page 203 of "The Wind." Compare and contrast how the authors resolve their stories. Use details from the text to support your answer. Write your answer below, on a separate sheet of paper, or in a new document.

Students demonstrate contextual understanding of Benchmark Vocabulary. Students read text closely and use text evidence in their written answers.

Name ______________________________

Writing

Narrative Writing: Use Research to Explore Theme Use what you have learned to do your own research and write a new fantasy or science fiction story. Perform your own research for a fantasy or science fiction story about space colonization.

Write your stories on a separate sheet of paper or start a new document.

Conventions

Use Strategies to Improve Expression

DIRECTIONS Rewrite each sentence to reflect proper subject/verb agreement.

1. We going to the pool later.

____

____

2. Frank my oldest brother.

____

____

3. That plate dirty, so I washed it.

____

____

4. Cecilia and Diana both getting good grades in science class.

____

____

5. You going to be at my house at 7:00, right?

____

____

Students write routinely for a range of tasks, purposes, and audiences. Students practice various conventions of standard English.

Name ______________________

Benchmark Vocabulary

DIRECTIONS Write a sentence using each word.

intrigued harrowing fluent

Write in Response to Reading

DIRECTIONS Reread pages 10, 11, 13, and 14. Based on this text, readers can infer that Margret and Hans were both courageous. Using text evidence, write a paragraph that tells which individual—Hans or Margret—shows more courage as the story begins. Write your answer below, on a separate sheet of paper, or in a new document.

Students demonstrate contextual understanding of Benchmark Vocabulary. Students read text closely and use text evidence in their written answers.

Name ______________________

Writing

Informative/Explanatory Writing: Write an Analysis of Text and Visual Features
Analyze the text and visual features of pages 3–15 of *The Journey That Saved Curious George*. Use your Three-Column Chart to help you organize and analyze the relationships between the text and visuals and how they help to develop the life story of Margret and H. A. Rey. Then write an analysis of how the writer uses a combination of words and visuals to "stitch together the fabric of their story" based on the purpose and features of a biography. Keep the following points in mind as you write your analysis:

- Consider how the writer uses both text and visuals to bring the two life stories together.
- Include examples from pages 3–15 to support your analysis. Quote the text as needed and include page numbers.
- Include examples from the text that were discussed in class and not discussed in class. Use a separate sheet of paper or start a new document.

Conventions

Punctuate Items in a Series

DIRECTIONS Rewrite each sentence to correctly punctuate the items in a series. Use commas to separate listed items and use semicolons to separate categories and items that already contain commas.

1. Don't forget to pack your pajamas socks toothbrush and toothpaste.

____

2. His family has taken vacations to Rome Italy Paris France and Beijing China.

____

3. We will visit family including my aunt uncle and cousins go to the art museum cathedral the famous market and the park and try some local dishes.

____

____

Students write routinely for a range of tasks, purposes, and audiences. Students practice various conventions of standard English.

Name ______________________________ Word Analysis

Figures of Speech: Expressions, Idioms, and Sayings

DIRECTIONS Match each expression, idiom, or saying with its figurative meaning.

1. lay your cards on the table	**a.** have a similar situation	**1.** ______
2. put it on the back burner	**b.** gain an advantage	**2.** ______
3. have an inside track	**c.** do not make it a priority	**3.** ______
4. be in the same boat	**d.** reveal all the facts	**4.** ______

DIRECTIONS Underline the phrase in each sentence that is an expression, idiom, or saying.

5. He's already jumping off the deep end by making a fancy dinner for ten people when he just learned how to cook.

6. We were leaving for a long-awaited camping trip when a surprise phone call pulled the rug out from under us.

7. When Cam didn't apply to more than one college, she put all her eggs into one basket.

8. It slipped his mind that he was supposed to take out the garbage that day.

DIRECTIONS Write the meaning of the underlined expression, idiom, or saying.

9. I'm going to throw in the towel for now because I can't get all my work done tonight.

____

10. Vic's winning the state spelling bee is nothing to sneeze at.

____

11. She's never been late before, so don't make a federal case this one time.

____

12. We told him to get off his high horse and stop bragging all the time.

____

Students apply grade-level word analysis skills.

Name ______________________________

Benchmark Vocabulary

DIRECTIONS Write a sentence using each word.

neutral regulations

____
____
____
____

Write in Response to Reading

Reread pages 30–36. Use text evidence to write an informative/explanatory paragraph that summarizes this section of the biography. Write your answer below, on a separate sheet of paper, or in a new document.

____
____
____
____
____
____
____
____
____
____
____
____

Students demonstrate contextual understanding of Benchmark Vocabulary. Students read text closely and use text evidence in their written answers.

Name ______________________________

Analyze Key Events

DIRECTIONS Using evidence from the text, answer the following questions about pages 16–36 from *The Journey That Saved Curious George.*

1. When the war began in 1939, the Reys react by leaving Paris and going to Château Feuga. Why might they feel safer here than in Paris, and how does this safety prove to be an illusion? How do these events help the author elaborate on the nature of the war?

____

____

____

____

2. On pages 27 and 35 of the text, the Reys twice prepare to "return home." In what ways does the proximity of the war affect their actions?

____

____

____

3. The Reys respond to the war with Germany by worrying about old friends and family. How do these emotions help the author illustrate life during war?

____

____

____

4. The Reys work as children's book authors. In what ways does the war affect their business?

____

____

____

Students analyze and respond to literary and informational text.

Name ____________________

Writing

Informative/Explanatory Writing: Research and Take Notes About An Individual
Use your completed Three-Column Chart to help you write a few good research questions that you can use to research Hans Reyersbach's early life in Germany. Remember that you are looking for information that could be used in a biography of Hans. Then conduct print and online research to find the information you need to answer your questions. Take detailed notes, by quoting or paraphrasing, to record your findings. Record bibliographic information about the source of each note. Use a separate sheet of paper or start a new document for each research question.

Conventions

Order of Adjectives Within Sentences In each sentence, circle the adjectives and underline the noun or pronoun that they describe. If the adjectives are in the correct order, write *Correct* on the line. If the order is incorrect, write the adjectives in the correct order on the line.

1. A strawberry, frozen, large yogurt is my favorite treat.

____

2. The many, small, polluted lakes in this area are terrible for swimming.

____

3. Rashida is looking for a large, rectangular, framed mirror for her bedroom.

____

4. Daniel said that this book retells a Native American, interesting, traditional story.

____

5. The sculptor made a clay, enormous, flattering, red statue of the town's founder.

____

Students write routinely for a range of tasks, purposes, and audiences. Students practice various conventions of standard English.

Name ___________________________________

DIRECTIONS Write a sentence using each word.

tempo relentless evacuation

Write in Response to Reading

DIRECTIONS Reread page 46 of *The Journey That Saved Curious George* and study the illustrations on the corresponding pages. How do the items that Hans and Margret decide to pack help you develop an understanding of the situation Parisians faced as they prepared to evacuate? Use textual and visual evidence to support your answer. Write your answer below, on a separate sheet of paper, or in a new document.

Students demonstrate contextual understanding of Benchmark Vocabulary. Students read text closely and use text evidence in their written answers.

Name ______________________

Sleuth Work

Major League Dreams

Tall, swaying palm trees line white sandy beaches in the Dominican Republic. Many tourists call it paradise. But for many Dominicans, life can be difficult. About 42 percent of the people live in poverty. Unemployment is high, and good jobs are hard to keep. As a result, many Dominicans dream of living in the United States. For young men with extra-large dreams, a ticket to the United States is often tied to a baseball bat.

Several great Major League Baseball players are Dominican. They include Albert Pujols, Starlin Castro, Jose Reyes, and Bartolo Colón, to name just a few. In fact, more baseball players who go to the major leagues come from the Dominican Republic than from any other country in the world outside of the United States.

Almost all of the major league teams have training camps in the baseball-crazed Dominican Republic. Their scouts scour the countryside for promising young players. Being invited to one of the camps can change a boy's life—even, perhaps, the life of his entire family. Boys who might have used brooms for bats and padded milk cartons for gloves receive proper equipment at training camps. They receive not only expert coaching but also food, medical care, and housing. The camps, which are also called academies, emphasize education as well. They teach skills useful on and off the field.

Thousands of talented young men have attended the camps, but the odds of finding fame and fortune are slim. Major League Baseball's website says that for every hundred players who make it to a training camp, only four or five ever make it to the big leagues. For each famous player, there are hundreds who lack the necessary abilities, determination to be the best, or just luck.

For those who come to the United States, the difficulties don't end on arrival. Learning a new language is a big hurdle to overcome. Living in a new place with a different culture requires an adjustment. Even ordering food in a restaurant is difficult. Some players find that adjusting to their new lives is harder than hitting a baseball out of the ballpark, yet they keep trying. With a chance of making it to the World Series, Dominicans who come to play baseball in the United States have to weigh the dreams and the challenges.

Students read text closely to determine what the text says.

Name ____________________

Gather Evidence Underline details about benefits players receive from attending training camps in the Dominican Republic. Write a list of these benefits.

____

____

Gather Evidence: Extend Your Ideas Review underlined details. Why might players view the camps as "paradise" like tourists view the Dominican Republic as "paradise"?

____

____

Ask Questions Circle the names of Dominican Major League Baseball players. Write three questions you might ask one of these players. Include at least one detail from the text in each question.

____

____

Ask Questions: Extend Your Ideas Based on the text, how might a player answer one of your questions? List reliable resources you could use to verify your answers.

____

____

Make Your Case Bracket sentences that provide evidence of the challenges players face when they arrive in the United States. Then, write a one-sentence summary.

____

____

Make Your Case: Extend Your Ideas Do you think Major League Baseball is doing enough to help players transition to life in the United States? Discuss your point of view with a partner and use details in the text to support your response.

____

____

Students read text closely to determine what the text says.

Name ______________________________

Writing

Informative/Explanatory Writing: Verify Biographical Information Identify five concrete details or events among your notes from Lesson 2 and verify the information for each by finding a second credible source describing the same information. For each item, write the information (detail or event) you verified; detail source information for the confirming source, including the title, author, publisher, date, and page numbers or Web site address (URL);. and write explanation of why you consider the source to be credible. Use a separate sheet of paper or start a new document.

Conventions

Use Linking Verbs

DIRECTIONS Write a sentence that uses a form or part of the given linking verb to link a subject to information about the subject.

1. (be) ______________________________

2. (seem) ______________________________

3. (become) ______________________________

4. (feel) ______________________________

5. (grow) ______________________________

Students write routinely for a range of tasks, purposes, and audiences. Students practice various conventions of standard English.

Name ____________________

Benchmark Vocabulary

DIRECTIONS Write a sentence using each word.

bedlam sufficient correspondence

Write in Response to Reading

DIRECTIONS The central idea of *The Journey That Saved Curious George* involves Margret and Hans Rey's courageous escape from Europe during World War II. Review the stages of their journey beginning on page 50. During which part of their escape did the Reys demonstrate the most courage and why? Use text evidence to write an opinion paragraph that describes this part of the journey and how Hans and Margret reacted with courage. Write your answer below, on a separate sheet of paper, or in a new document.

Students demonstrate contextual understanding of Benchmark Vocabulary. Students read text closely and use text evidence in their written answers.

Name ____________________

Determine a Central Idea

DIRECTIONS Using evidence from the text, answer the following questions about pages 50–71 from *The Journey That Saved Curious George*.

1. What information related to the setting on pages 63 and 66 illustrates the central idea that the Reys maintain courage despite facing many obstacles over the course of their journey?

2. What text evidence on page 66 emphasizes how the Reys demonstrate courage as they wait for passage to America?

3. One element of their journey is how Hans and Margret do almost everything together. In what ways might this partnership strengthen the courage of each individual?

Students analyze and respond to literary and informational text.

Name ____________________

Informative/Explanatory Writing: Write an Outline Organize your research findings from the previous lesson using an outline of Hans Reyersbach's early life in Germany. Classify the information according to a central idea about different time periods or influential events, and use these categories as your main outline topics. Use the Main Idea graphic organizer to help you develop and organize your ideas, concepts, and information for your outline. Your outline should include main topic headings that identify different time period or event categories and have a parallel structure. They should be correctly formatted using roman numerals for main topics, capital letters for subtopics, and numbers for supporting details. They should also include any visuals or other media that you may have found in your research. Use a separate sheet of paper or start a new document.

Participles

DIRECTIONS Underline the participle in each sentence. On the line, write *adjective* if the participle is used as an adjective. Write *verb* if the participle is used to make a verb form.

1. Toby is fixing the brakes on his bicycle by himself. ____________
2. The writing class gave a presentation at the library. ____________
3. Today, several professionals are visiting the school to talk about their careers. ____________
4. I knew you had brought your dog when I saw his leash. ____________
5. There was trash all over the floor because the trash bag had broken. ____________
6. The acting workshop ended with a lively performance. ____________

Students write routinely for a range of tasks, purposes, and audiences. Students practice various conventions of standard English.

Name ______________________________

Benchmark Vocabulary

DIRECTIONS Write a sentence using each word.

sabotage eviction uprooting

____

____

____

____

____

____

Write in Response to Reading

DIRECTIONS Reread pages 13–15. On page 13, the author explains Executive Order 9066. What happened because of this new law? How did it affect the author and her family? Use text evidence to write an explanatory paragraph. Write your answer below, on a separate sheet of paper, or in a new document.

____

____

____

____

____

____

Students demonstrate contextual understanding of Benchmark Vocabulary. Students read text closely and use text evidence in their written answers.

Name ______________________________

Writing

Informative/Explanatory Writing: Write an Introduction to a Biography Use your planning notes to help you write an introductory paragraph for a biography that introduces readers to Yoshiko Uchida. Remember that to effectively introduce a topic for a biography, you should grab the interest of the audience with the first sentence(s), introduce and accurately describe the individual, and introduce your central idea about the individual or her life.

Make sure to add relevant details from the text when introducing and describing Uchida, including facts, examples, and definitions. You may conduct additional research about Uchida if necessary.

Conventions

Prepositions and Prepositional Phrases

DIRECTIONS Write a sentence to use each given preposition as part of a prepositional phrase.

1. to ______________________________
2. about ______________________________
3. behind ______________________________
4. during ______________________________
5. despite ______________________________

Students write routinely for a range of tasks, purposes, and audiences. Students practice various conventions of standard English.

Name ______________________________

Benchmark Vocabulary

DIRECTIONS Write a sentence using each word.

degrading naively incarcerating

____

____

____

____

____

____

Write in Response to Reading

DIRECTIONS Reread pages 22–23. The narrator explains that throughout the family's move to the camps, the people never considered protesting or fighting against the evacuation. Do you think that citizens of Japanese ancestry should have resisted their internment? Use text evidence to write an opinion paragraph that explains your point of view. Write your answer below, on a separate sheet of paper, or in a new document.

____

____

____

____

____

____

Students demonstrate contextual understanding of Benchmark Vocabulary. Students read text closely and use text evidence in their written answers.

Name ______________________________

Informative/Explanatory Writing: Write About an Event Using Cause-and-Effect Use your planning notes and text evidence to help you write several paragraphs that include a cause-and-effect structure to explain a key event or events impacting Yoshiko Uchida's life during World War II. The cause-and-effect structure should highlight the event's full significance, based on the text and your prior knowledge of this time period. Choose your words carefully to convey the cause-and-effect relationships that you identified. If necessary, you will be given extra time to conduct research and check any inferences or conclusions in the next lesson. Remember, classification may be an additional appropriate strategy for organizing your paragraphs. Use a separate sheet of paper or start a new document.

Prepositional Phrases as Adjectives

DIRECTIONS Read each sentence and pick a noun to modify with a prepositional phrase. Underline the noun. Then rewrite the sentence to include a prepositional phrase that adds information about the underlined noun.

1. The friends met at the park and spent several hours talking.

____

2. Allison's brother recommended bringing a book on the trip.

____

3. Our class is creating a Web site and each student will create one Web page.

____

4. Dean rearranged the order and e-mailed the new list.

____

5. For their first long hike, each camper carried plenty of water and a compass.

____

Students write routinely for a range of tasks, purposes, and audiences. Students practice various conventions of standard English.

Name ______________________________

Word Analysis

Greek and Latin Roots *tele*, *medi*, *funct*, *struct*

Word Bank

construction	function	intermediary	mediocre	telegram
destructive	functionaries	medial	semifunctional	telephone
dysfunction	instructions	mediate	substructure	televise

DIRECTIONS Write each word from the Word Bank next to its meaning.

1. of only moderate quality — 1. ______________
2. go-between — 2. ______________
3. partially capable of operating — 3. ______________
4. orders or directions — 4. ______________
5. performance that is not normal — 5. ______________
6. the act of building — 6. ______________
7. officials — 7. ______________
8. device used to speak over distances — 8. ______________
9. to act between opposing sides — 9. ______________
10. to send pictures by television — 10. ______________
11. the purpose intended for a thing — 11. ______________
12. causing ruin — 12. ______________
13. message written from signals received over a distance — 13. ______________
14. something that forms a foundation — 14. ______________
15. mean — 15. ______________

Students apply grade-level word analysis skills.

Name ______________________________

Benchmark Vocabulary

DIRECTIONS Write a sentence using each word.

prejudice   hysteria   mitigate

____

____

____

____

____

____

Write in Response to Reading

DIRECTIONS In the epilogue, the author outlines the steps the U.S. government has taken to make amends for the unconstitutional treatment of Japanese Americans during World War II. Use text evidence to write an opinion paragraph that tells whether you believe the government has done enough for this group of people. Write your answer below, on a separate sheet of paper, or in a new document.

____

____

____

____

____

____

____

Students demonstrate contextual understanding of Benchmark Vocabulary. Students read text closely and use text evidence in their written answers.

Name ____________________

Reading Analysis

Development of Ideas

DIRECTIONS Using evidence from the text, answer the following questions about pages 24–25 from *The Invisible Thread.*

1. How does the timing of the passage of the Redress Bill contrast to the timing of the forced evacuations of Japanese Americans? What does the author's use of the phrase "at last" on page 25 suggest about her point of view on this timing?

2. What does the author's use of the word *footnote* suggest about her point of view in the epilogue as contrasted with the remainder of the text?

3. The author notes in the epilogue that she finds it hard to believe that the internment of Japanese Americans actually happened in the United States. How does this reaction compare with her thoughts in 1942?

4. In the epilogue, the author notes that President Carter refers to "war hysteria" as one of the reasons for the Japanese Americans' evacuations. How do President Carter's words and actions contrast with President Roosevelt's on page 13?

Students analyze and respond to literary and informational text.

Name ____________________

Writing

Informative/Explanatory Writing: Develop a Topic Using Research Conduct research to find more information about the internment of Yoshiko Uchida and her family that will help you to describe specific events in this period of her life. Then write several paragraphs that inform your audience about these events. Include relevant, revealing examples of specific events, concrete details, and quotes from Uchida and her family members to make the information more vivid and engaging, so your writing reads more like a story than an encyclopedia entry about Yoshiko Uchida. Record detailed bibliographic information for all of the sources you use.
Use a separate sheet of paper or start a new document.

Conventions

Prepositional Phrases as Adverbs

DIRECTIONS In each section, circle the verb and underline the prepositional phrase that modifies it. On the line, write *Where, When*, or *How* to identify what information the prepositional phrase adds about the action named by the verb.

1. Jan sat in between Deborah and Mai, her best friends.

   ____

2. Jogender brought and shared some snacks baked by his grandmother.

   ____

3. The school served hamburgers and salad for lunch.

   ____

4. I'll give you a ride home if you meet me in the parking lot.

   ____

5. Before recess, we grabbed our jackets since it was cold out.

   ____

Students write routinely for a range of tasks, purposes, and audiences. Students practice various conventions of standard English.

Name ______________________________

Benchmark Vocabulary

DIRECTIONS Write a sentence using each word.

regulations degrading prejudice

Write in Response to Reading

DIRECTIONS Based on the authors' use of narration in *The Journey That Saved Curious George* and *The Invisible Thread,* which perspective, first-person or third-person, is more effective at engaging readers and giving information about World War II and central ideas relating to courage? Compare and contrast evidence from both texts to write a paragraph in which you explain your response. Write your answer below, on a separate sheet of paper, or in a new document.

Students demonstrate contextual understanding of Benchmark Vocabulary. Students read text closely and use text evidence in their written answers.

Name ______________________

Compare and Contrast Texts

DIRECTIONS Using evidence from the texts, answer the following questions about *The Journey That Saved Curious George* and *The Invisible Thread.*

1. Why might the narration of *The Invisible Thread* contain an angry tone that is not present in the narration of *The Journey That Saved Curious George?*

2. The authors of both *The Journey That Saved Curious George* and *The Invisible Thread* use primary sources to support their ideas and develop point of view. How do the primary sources differ and to what effect?

3. The authors of both *The Journey That Saved Curious George* and *The Invisible Thread* base their narratives on events that took place more than 50 years ago. How do the authors convey the reliability of the information?

Students analyze and respond to literary and informational text.

Name ____

Writing

Informative/Explanatory Writing: Add Transitions to Connect Ideas Review your partner's feedback on your biography about Yoshiko Uchida and check your draft for missing transitions yourself. Then add appropriate transitions where necessary between sentences, paragraphs, and the following three sections you have written so far: the introductory paragraph, the key event and its causes and effects, and the additional information about specific internment events. Remember, your goal is to clarify the relationships between ideas and create one coherent, unified text that reads smoothly. Write or type a clean version of your biography with the transitions included. Use a separate sheet of paper or start a new document.

Conventions

Subject-Verb Agreement with Intervening Prepositional Phrases

DIRECTIONS Circle the subject and write the correct form of the verb to complete the sentence.

1. The schedule of events ____________ (includes, include) a concert in the evening.
2. Tickets for the concert ____________ (costs, cost) twenty dollars each.
3. The seats directly behind the podium ____________ (offers, offer) the best view of the orchestra.
4. Let's see how long the students in line ____________ (has been, have been) waiting.
5. All the advertisements in the concert program ____________ (is, are) for local businesses.
6. Next year, Mr. Peña's class of sixth graders ____________ (is going, are going) to sell concert tickets to fundraise.

Students write routinely for a range of tasks, purposes, and audiences. Students practice various conventions of standard English.

Name ______________________________

Benchmark Vocabulary

DIRECTIONS Write a sentence using each word.

prohibiting compensation impartial

____

____

____

____

____

____

Write in Response to Reading

DIRECTIONS Review Amendment V in the Bill of Rights. This amendment includes four related ideas concerning criminal justice. Use text evidence to write an informative paragraph that summarizes the central ideas in Amendment V. In your paragraph, discuss how specific technical language enables you to interpret these ideas about justice. Write your answer below, on a separate sheet of paper, or in a new document.

____

____

____

____

____

____

____

Students demonstrate contextual understanding of Benchmark Vocabulary. Students read text closely and use text evidence in their written answers.

Name ______________________________

Writing

Informative/Explanatory Writing: Write Using Precise Language Conduct research and use credible sources to gather information about how the Bill of Rights was drafted. Identify technical terms that you should use to write formally about this topic and then write several paragraphs to provide background information about drafting the Bill of Rights. Use precise language, including the technical terms you found. Remember to write in a formal style. Use a separate sheet of paper or start a new document.

Conventions

Pronoun-Antecedent Agreement

DIRECTIONS Write the correct pronoun to complete each sentence. Circle the antecedent.

1. Charlie is looking forward to the day when ____________ is old enough to vote.
2. Pam and Cindy said that ____________ will take turns recording the debates.
3. Our class will watch each presidential debate the day after ____________ is broadcast on TV.
4. The candidates will answer questions texted to the station, so we can ask ____________ about important issues.
5. If you ask her, ____________ will probably give you an honest answer.
6. Ben texted the question, "My class wants to know if you can tell ____________ what you will do about global warming."

Students write routinely for a range of tasks, purposes, and audiences. Students practice various conventions of standard English.

Name ______________________

Benchmark Vocabulary

DIRECTIONS Write a sentence using each word.

incarcerating prohibiting

Write in Response to Reading

On page 8 of *The Invisible Thread,* Kay comments: "We're prisoners in our own home. . . . The police even broke in and searched our house while we were out." Use text evidence to write a paragraph that compares and contrasts this situation with one or more amendments in the Bill of Rights. Write your answer below, on a separate sheet of paper, or in a new document.

Students demonstrate contextual understanding of Benchmark Vocabulary. Students read text closely and use text evidence in their written answers.

Name ______________________

Compare and Contrast Texts

DIRECTIONS Using evidence from the texts, answer the following questions about *The Invisible Thread* and the Bill of Rights.

1. Both Amendment V and the author of *The Invisible Thread* agree that a person should not be held for a crime without due process of law. How do the authors differ in the language they use to present this idea?

____

____

____

2. Both Amendment V and *The Invisible Thread* address personal financial loss due to government action. How do the authors differ in addressing this idea?

____

____

____

____

3. In Amendment V, the words "except in cases [of] … public danger" are included as an exception to the right that no person shall be held without due process. How does *The Invisible Thread* illustrate that this part of Amendment V should not have been applied to Japanese Americans during World War II?

____

____

____

Students analyze and respond to literary and informational text.

Name ______________________________

Writing

Informative/Explanatory Writing: Write a Conclusion for a Biography Continue writing your biography about Yoshiko Uchida's life during World War II. Use your planning notes to help you write a concluding section of one or more paragraphs that follows from the information you presented. Remember, a satisfying and effective conclusion for this short biography will do the following:

- Briefly inform about an aspect of Yoshiko Uchida's later life that is relevant to the central idea.
- Remind readers of main points and reasserts the central idea.
- Provide a closing thought about the larger significance or meaning of this biography for readers to reflect on.

Add your conclusion to the end of your draft and continue on a new sheet of paper, if needed, or continue in the same document file.

Conventions

Pronoun-Antecedent Agreement in Number

DIRECTIONS In each sentence, circle the antecedent the underlined pronoun refers to. Write *singular* or *plural* on the line to show why the pronoun and antecedent agree.

1. Anthony decided that <u>he</u> would make a list of the ten most influential people in the world. ____________

2. He got the idea from a magazine that publishes <u>its</u> own list of "movers and shakers" every year. ____________

3. The magazine's editors suggest people to include and then <u>they</u> vote on all of the candidates. ____________

4. The editors call the winners to tell <u>them</u> they are included on the list. ____________

5. Tina and I made <u>our</u> own list of influential people. ____________

6. The business leader asked to write <u>her</u> own biography for the magazine. ____________

Students write routinely for a range of tasks, purposes, and audiences. Students practice various conventions of standard English.

Name ________________________________

Benchmark Vocabulary

DIRECTIONS Write a sentence using each word.

adversity   detainment   confined

Write in Response to Reading

DIRECTIONS Reread this quotation about Yoshiko Uchida from page 31 of *Stories of Courage*: "Through her writing, she taught young people to never use labels to separate themselves from one another, and to face life's challenges with grace and hope." Use text evidence to write an explanatory paragraph that analyzes how specific key events in Uchida's life enabled her to teach these lessons about courage to others. Write your answer below, on a separate sheet of paper, or in a new document.

Students demonstrate contextual understanding of Benchmark Vocabulary. Students read text closely and use text evidence in their written answers.

Name ______________________________

Informative/Explanatory Writing: Prewrite a Biography Plan and prewrite a biography about a well-known author other than Margret Rey, H. A. Rey, and Yoshiko Uchida. Complete the following steps and write down all of your decisions, in addition to taking notes on your research findings:

- Select a subject for your biography. Consider that you are writing to inform a general audience that includes your classmates.
- Conduct initial research about the author you chose. Gather and record basic background information about his or her life and accomplishments.
- Record detailed bibliographic information about all of the sources you use.
- Write a list of research questions about your author to identify any personal information you are missing about his or her experiences or character.

If you need help organizing your research findings, consider creating a time line or Sequence graphic organizer of your author's life. You will use the questions you write to research answers in the next lesson. Use a separate sheet of paper or start a new document.

Correct Inappropriate Shifts in Pronoun Number

DIRECTIONS In each sentence, circle the pronoun and its antecedent. If the pronoun and antecedent do not agree, write a pronoun that can replace the one used.

1. Leia's favorite books are about famous leaders and what they experienced during times of crisis. ____________
2. Many biographies about Margaret Thatcher describe their childhood in detail. ____________
3. Since they're brothers, Tom and Ben are writing a biography about his grandfather together. ____________
4. If people want to write a biography, he have to be good researchers. ____________
5. A biography writer can ask their subject for an interview to gather information. ____________

Students write routinely for a range of tasks, purposes, and audiences. Students practice various conventions of standard English.

Name ____

Word Analysis

Multiple-Meaning Words

	Spelling	Pronunciation	Meaning	Examples
Homophone	different	same	different	*ate, eight*
Homograph	same	different	different	*written record, record a song*
Homonym	same	same	different	*wishing well, feeling well*

DIRECTIONS Circle the two homophones in each sentence. Use the chart for help.

1. During the martial arts class, the fire marshal came to investigate the building.
2. Please compliment the chef for the tasty appetizers that complement the main course.
3. Ginny was just finishing her carrot cake when Takao proposed with a 24-karat gold ring.
4. The boss constantly praised his assistants because they always provided the assistance he needed.

DIRECTIONS Identify the two words in each sentence that are either homographs or homonyms. Write each word on the line followed by the word *homograph* or *homonym.*

5. People who saw the magician saw a woman in two were in disbelief.

____

6. When it's hot, the fans bring their portable fans to cool themselves off.

____

7. My aunt who's an invalid received a new medical card that replaced her old, invalid one.

____

Students apply grade-level word analysis skills.

Name ____________________

Benchmark Vocabulary

DIRECTIONS Write a sentence using each word.

typical willpower treacherous

Write in Response to Reading

DIRECTIONS Consider this direct statement of the author's point of view about Kyle Maynard: "His personal philosophy is to make no excuses because there are no such things as barriers," page 33. Use text evidence to write an opinion paragraph critiquing how well the author supports this point of view in the text. Write your answer below, on a separate sheet of paper, or in a new document.

Students demonstrate contextual understanding of Benchmark Vocabulary. Students read text closely and use text evidence in their written answers.

Name ______________________________

Writing

Informative/Explanatory Writing: Record and Organize Information Use your research questions from the previous lesson to conduct research and organize your findings about your chosen author. Complete the following tasks:

- Use credible print and online sources to find answers to your research questions, and take notes to record your findings.
- Create a reference list of your sources and verify the accuracy of information from each source.
- Choose a strategy of organization for the information you collected. Then organize your notes in an outline or Sequence graphic organizer under appropriate headings.
- Select possible photos or graphics to support your writing, and name these in the outline or Sequence graphic organizer to show where they will be used.

Use a separate sheet of paper or start a new document.

Conventions

Pronoun-Antecedent Agreement in Person

DIRECTIONS In each sentence, circle the pronoun and its antecedent. If the pronoun and antecedent do not agree, write a pronoun that can replace the one used.

1. David has never hiked in the woods before, so she is going to follow the guide closely. ____________
2. The trail guides will count everyone in his group at each rest stop, to make sure no one gets lost. ____________
3. For our camping trip, just two tents should be enough for me and three other people. ____________
4. Jenn and Alyssa know this trail very well and are happy to share your knowledge of landmarks with others. ____________
5. The ranger explained the park's rules about littering and has asked that everyone obey us. ____________

Students write routinely for a range of tasks, purposes, and audiences. Students practice various conventions of standard English.

Name ______________________________

Benchmark Vocabulary

DIRECTIONS Write a sentence using each word.

outspoken injustices anonymous

____

____

____

____

____

____

Write in Response to Reading

DIRECTIONS Reread the last paragraph of "The Fearless Schoolgirl" on page 37: "Despite all the increased visibility, Malala was not afraid for herself. Instead, she feared for her father's life, especially because he already had received death threats." Use text evidence to write an explanatory paragraph that tells how *this* paragraph helps the author elaborate further on Yousafzai's character traits. Write your answer below, on a separate sheet of paper, or in a new document.

____

____

____

____

____

____

Students demonstrate contextual understanding of Benchmark Vocabulary. Students read text closely and use text evidence in their written answers.

Name ______________________________

A New Home for Kabanda

Every morning when Olivia was hurrying to clean cages at the zoo's monkey house, she passed by the small elephant enclosure where Kabanda lived. Often, she heard him speaking to her as she passed. He typically made a soft rumbling sound that Olivia was certain meant "I'm lonely."

Olivia knew that elephants are very social animals, and Kabanda had been all alone in his enclosure for almost two years now, ever since his mate Adana had died. So, every morning, Olivia made sure she answered back in her most soothing voice, "I know, Kabanda, I know."

Some mornings Olivia would notice that Kabanda just swayed a little and bobbed his head. She knew this behavior was common in elephants held in captivity for long periods. She had read articles about how they began to show signs of sadness, even depression. Olivia would tell Kabanda, "So many people care about you. Change is coming, Kabanda!"

And it was. Olivia was not the only one who felt bad for the huge animal isolated in its tiny, cramped space. Kabanda had been in the news ever since his companion had died. The old zoo where he lived and Olivia worked had been built before people fully understood and sympathized with the needs of animals in captivity.

The elephant enclosure drew the most criticism because much of the public now believed that elephants needed vast natural expanses, with acres and acres of land. However, Kabanda was confined to a half-acre or so. Some zoo visitors interpreted the loud trumpeting sound Kabanda sometimes made as a cry of misery. Others said that there was no such thing as a good zoo for elephants. Elephants, they argued, needed entire wildlife parks, where several animal families could roam around and find their own food.

Kabanda never got the wildlife park, but his suffering at the old zoo didn't last much longer. One morning Olivia stopped at his enclosure, pointed west beyond the city boundaries, and said, "Kabanda, I have the best news for you. You're moving to a new zoo over that hill. It's much bigger, and best of all, there are other elephants. You will not be alone." Of course, Olivia knew that Kabanda couldn't understand what she was saying. But when the elephant suddenly lifted his head and trumpeted, Olivia wondered if maybe he understood her after all.

Students read text closely to determine what the text says.

Name ______________________________

Sleuth Work

Gather Evidence Underline sentences in the text that show how Olivia feels about Kabanda. How does Olivia express her feelings toward the elephant?

Gather Evidence: Extend Your Ideas Based on the underlined sentences, briefly describe the feelings Olivia expresses toward Kabanda.

Ask Questions Circle words that describe Kabanda's enclosure. Write three questions you could ask a large-animal veterinarian about the effect living in such a space might have on an animal such as an elephant. Include details from the text in your questions.

Ask Questions: Extend Your Ideas Based on the text, how might the veterinarian answer your questions? List examples of reliable resources you could use to verify your answers.

Make Your Case Bracket sentences that provide evidence about how Kabanda responds to Olivia's communications. Do you believe that the elephant understands Olivia? Cite details to support your judgment.

Make Your Case: Extend Your Ideas What kinds of communication do you believe are possible between animals and humans? Discuss your viewpoint with a partner, and use details from the text to support your response.

Students read text closely to determine what the text says.

Name ____

Writing

Informative/Explanatory Writing: Write a First Draft of a Biography Write a first draft of the biography you planned in the two previous lessons. Your main goal in writing a draft is to tell the complete life story from beginning to end. Try to write without stopping and don't worry about making your writing perfect; you will have time to revise and edit your draft in later lessons. As you write your draft, refer to your outline or Sequence graphic organizer for the headings and information you will address in each section. Include references about graphic or visual elements you plan to use. Keep your central idea in mind and write in a formal but engaging style. Use a separate sheet of paper or start a new document.

Conventions

Correct Pronoun Shifts in Number in Sentences

DIRECTIONS In each sentence, circle the pronoun and its antecedent. Then write the correct pronoun that agrees with the antecedent.

1. In some countries, girls have to stand up for her right to have an education. _______
2. The school invited the activists to come and talk to their students. _______
3. Andy went to a demonstration for new environmental laws to show support for their sister, the organizer. _______
4. Sophie and her brother made signs that he both could carry while marching with the protestors. _______
5. The news team will record Saturday's demonstration for their next broadcast. _______

Students write routinely for a range of tasks, purposes, and audiences. Students practice various conventions of standard English.

Name ______________________________

Benchmark Vocabulary

DIRECTIONS Write a sentence using each word.

crisis ravaged extreme

____

____

____

____

____

____

Write in Response to Reading

DIRECTIONS Reread the third paragraph on page 40, beginning "In the chaos, John lost track of his family." Then, reread the last paragraph on page 42. Use text evidence to write an explanatory paragraph that tells how the author uses the central idea of family to illustrate her point of view regarding John Bul Dau's courage. Write your answer below, on a separate sheet of paper, or in a new document.

____

____

____

____

____

____

____

____

____

Students demonstrate contextual understanding of Benchmark Vocabulary. Students read text closely and use text evidence in their written answers.

Name ______________________________

Point of View

DIRECTIONS Using evidence from the text, answer the following questions about pages 40–43 from *Stories of Courage.*

1. On page 40, the author describes Bul Dau's escape as both "harrowing" and "brave." What do these word choices convey about the author's point of view on the event?

____

____

____

2. Reread the second paragraph on page 40. How does the author's use of sensory language such as "sticky heat" and "sudden whistling" help her convey her point of view about the terror of the event?

____

____

____

3. On page 42, what view does the author hold of the decision of the 20,000 boys to walk a thousand miles to safety? How do you know?

____

____

____

4. At the end of the selection, the author discusses John's wife and children. Does the author view Bul Dau's role as a father positively or negatively? Explain.

____

____

____

Students analyze and respond to literary and informational text.

Name ______________________________________

Writing

Informative/Explanatory Writing: Revise a Biography First Draft Review and revise the first draft of the biography you are writing. Your goal is to ensure that the draft clearly and accurately represents information about your subject in an interesting way. Work with a partner to review each other's drafts and share and discuss your feedback, then review and revise your own draft. Give particular attention to clarifying unclear or vague language choices and adding appropriate transitions where necessary. Check that all information presented about the individual is relevant, accurate, and informative. Use a separate sheet of paper or start a new document to make your revisions.

Conventions

Correct Pronoun Shifts in Number in Paragraphs

DIRECTIONS Read the paragraph. Write the antecedent for each underlined pronoun on the line below. If the pronoun and antecedent do not agree, write a pronoun that can replace the incorrect pronoun used. If the pronoun and antecedent do agree, write the word *Correct*.

Robyn told me about two biographies that (1) <u>we</u> read. The first biography was about Amelia Earhart, a pioneering female air pilot. The story's mysterious ending was Robyn's favorite part, and (2) <u>we</u> wondered if (3) <u>they</u> would ever be resolved. After class, (4) <u>she</u> and (5) <u>their</u> teacher discussed the difficulty of flying over an ocean. (6) <u>He</u> both agreed that the lack of landmarks would terrify (7) <u>her</u>, but pilots must be used to (8) <u>it</u>.

1. we ____________________
2. we ____________________
3. they ____________________
4. she ____________________
5. their ____________________
6. He ____________________
7. her ____________________
8. it ____________________

Students write routinely for a range of tasks, purposes, and audiences. Students practice various conventions of standard English.

Name ____________________

Benchmark Vocabulary

DIRECTIONS Write a sentence using each word.

eviction crisis

____

____

____

____

Write in Response to Reading

DIRECTIONS Reread page 25 of *The Invisible Thread.* Then reread the profiles of Malala Yousafzai, John Bul Dau, and Yoshiko Uchida in *Stories of Courage*. Use text evidence to write one paragraph comparing and contrasting how these people showed courage and work to make sure injustices never happen again. Write your answer below, on a separate sheet of paper, or in a new document.

____

____

____

____

____

____

Students demonstrate contextual understanding of Benchmark Vocabulary. Students read text closely and use text evidence in their written answers.

Name ___________________________________

Compare and Contrast

DIRECTIONS Using evidence from the texts, answer the following questions about *The Invisible Thread* and *Stories of Courage*.

1. How do the authors of *The Invisible Thread* and *Stories of Courage* contrast in their presentation of Uchida's happy childhood?

2. How do the authors of *The Invisible Thread* and *Stories of Courage* contrast in their presentations of Uchida's success as a student?

3. How do *The Invisible Thread* and *Stories of Courage* differ in their presentation of the condition of living quarters at Tanforan Assembly Center?

4. How do the authors of *The Invisible Thread* and *Stories of Courage* use different portions of the Japanese American internment experience to tell their stories?

Students analyze and respond to literary and informational text.

Name ______________________________________

Writing

Informative/Explanatory Writing: Edit and Proofread a Revised Draft Edit and proofread your revised drafts for your biography of an author. Carefully read and edit your draft for clarity first and then proofread for mistakes in spelling, grammar, punctuation, and capitalization. Do a separate read-through of your entire text, line-by-line, to focus on finding and correcting problems with pronoun-antecedent agreement, such as shifts in pronoun number and person and misspelled proper nouns and technical or subject-specific words. Use a separate sheet of paper or start a new document.

Conventions

Correct Pronoun Shifts in Person in Paragraphs

DIRECTIONS Read the following paragraph. Write the antecedent for each underlined pronoun on the line below. If the pronoun and antecedent do not agree in person, write a pronoun that can replace the one used. If the pronoun and antecedent do agree, write the word *Correct*.

Nicholas is writing a biography about (1) her grandmother. He will interview (2) her with a list of questions that he wrote. Nicholas is particularly interested in (3) his grandmother's childhood because (4) he spent some of her childhood in South Korea. Her father was an army officer stationed at the military base near Seoul, and (5) she and (6) her siblings all went to an American school on the base for five years. Nicholas knows that his grandmother is proud of (7) himself for having learned to speak Korean during her time there, and (8) he hopes she will teach him.

1. her ____________________
2. her ____________________
3. his ____________________
4. he ____________________
5. she ____________________
6. her ____________________
7. himself ____________________
8. he ____________________

Students write routinely for a range of tasks, purposes, and audiences. Students practice various conventions of standard English.

Name ______________________________

Benchmark Vocabulary

DIRECTIONS Write a sentence using each word.

relentless willpower

____

____

____

____

Write in Response to Reading

Reread page 46 of *The Journey That Saved Curious George*. Also reread details about John Bul Dau's escape on pages 40–42 in *Stories of Courage*. Use text evidence to write a paragraph comparing and contrasting how the events and visuals help the authors elaborate on the traits of the individuals. Write your answer below, on a separate sheet of paper, or in a new document.

____

____

____

____

____

____

____

____

____

Students demonstrate contextual understanding of Benchmark Vocabulary. Students read text closely and use text evidence in their written answers.

Name ______________________________

Writing

Informative/Explanatory Writing: Publish and Present a Biography Publish your biography of an author by creating, formatting, and adding images or multimedia elements to your clean, final draft from the previous lesson. Include a title and your name; visuals and/or multimedia elements to support your writing; a title, caption, and credit line for each image or multimedia element; and a list of references. Use a separate sheet of paper or start a new document. In your oral presentation, incorporate a supporting visual display and/or audio. You may reuse visuals that you added to your published paper. Remember to speak clearly and loudly and engage the audience with eye contact and your supporting visuals. Practice your delivery with a partner.

Conventions

Spell Correctly

DIRECTIONS Underline the misspelled word in each sentence. Spell the word correctly and write it on the line. Use a print, digital, or online dictionary to check your spelling.

1. Becoming the first female mayor of the city is a major acomplishmint.

    ____

2. As president of her class, she demonstrated a capibility for government.

    ____

3. His parents are imigrents from Russia who moved here before he was born.

    ____

4. Our family tree shows that we are dissendents of Thomas Jefferson.

    ____

5. A filanthropist is someone who gives time or donations to improve the welfare of others.

    ____

Students write routinely for a range of tasks, purposes, and audiences. Students practice various conventions of standard English.

Name ______________________________

Shades of Meaning

Word Bank

cruel	periodic	commotion	courteous	lessen

DIRECTIONS Write the word from the Word Bank with the shade of meanings that best fits in each set of words.

1. civil, ______________, polite, friendly
2. decrease, ______________, shrink, diminish
3. tough, strict, mean, ______________
4. infrequent, occasional, ______________, regular
5. ______________, unrest, disturbance, rebellion

DIRECTIONS Write the better word choice for each sentence.

6. The bread served at the restaurant was so (different, diverse) that I had never tasted anything like it before. ______________
7. A light (drizzle, rain) might dampen the mood a bit, but I think we should go ahead with the nature walk. ______________
8. Talia and her friends hope that their fundraiser will (heighten, multiply) the number of donations. ______________
9. He decided to take his girlfriend on a romantic moonlit (stroll, saunter) before he proposed. ______________
10. During the war, some people tried to flee into (indifferent, neutral) countries such as Switzerland. ______________
11. People were worried that things would get worse in the months ahead because of the (brewing, seething) conflict. ______________
12. All their children's books are filled with (lighthearted, hysterical) stories of mischievous animals. ______________
13. The teacher wanted students to feel (knowledgeable, smart) for their test on Friday. ______________
14. I spent all weekend preparing for my (travels, movement). ______________
15. The number of students who want to join the team is (increasing, intensifying).

____

Students apply grade-level word analysis skills.

Name ____________________

Benchmark Vocabulary

DIRECTIONS Write a sentence using each word.

evacuation uprooting adversity

Write in Response to Reading

DIRECTIONS Reread the Fifth Amendment of the Bill of Rights on page 45 of the *Text Collection* and pages 22–23 of *The Invisible Thread.* Use evidence from both texts to explain how the government deprived Japanese Americans of their rights and freedoms during World War II. Then describe the importance of these basic rights based on your interpretation of the texts. Write your answer below, on a separate sheet of paper, or in a new document.

Students demonstrate contextual understanding of Benchmark Vocabulary. Students read text closely and use text evidence in their written answers.

Name ______________________________ Reading Analysis

Central Ideas

DIRECTIONS Using evidence from the texts, answer the following questions about *The Journey That Saved Curious George, The Invisible Thread,* the Bill of Rights, and *Stories of Courage.*

1. How do both *The Journey That Saved Curious George* and the Bill of Rights support the central idea that freedom is important?

2. In *Stories of Courage,* how do both Malala Yousafzai and John Bul Dau risk their lives to gain freedom?

3. How do *The Journey That Saved Curious George, The Invisible Thread,* and *Stories of Courage* illustrate the central idea that freedom is not necessarily guaranteed?

Students analyze and respond to literary and informational text.

Name ______________________________

Writing

Informative/Explanatory Writing: Write a Paragraph Based on Research Use your Web A graphic organizer and planning notes to research and explore different definitions relating to your chosen term—*courage* or *freedom*. Research and refer to definitions presented in a variety of genres and types of writing, in both print and digital formats, including the texts for this module. Then write a formal paragraph providing your own definition of *courage* or *freedom* based on ideas from this module's texts and your additional research. Use a separate sheet of paper or start a new document.

Conventions

Use Standard English

DIRECTIONS Underline the use of nonstandard English in each sentence. Rewrite each sentence on the line below to use standard English.

1. I couldn't see nothing at the game because the people in front of me were standing on their chairs.

____

____

2. Tim finished his homework more faster than I did.

____

3. How much extra hot dogs do we hafta buy for the picnic?

____

4. Us and some other players are gonna ask if we can have an extra practice on Saturday.

____

5. Them don't appreciate all the effort and time it tooked to set up the tournament.

____

Students write routinely for a range of tasks, purposes, and audiences. Students practice various conventions of standard English.

Name ____________________

Benchmark Vocabulary

DIRECTIONS Write a sentence using each word.

discrimination injustices

Write in Response to Reading

DIRECTIONS Reread "Finding the Story" on page 3 in *The Journey That Saved Curious George.* Reread the introductory section on page 27 in *Stories of Courage.* Reread page 25 of *The Invisible Thread.* Finally, reread the introduction to the Bill of Rights on page 44. Use text evidence to write an explanatory paragraph comparing and contrasting how these sections relate to the overall presentation of topics and ideas in each text. Write your answer below, on a separate sheet of paper, or in a new document.

Students demonstrate contextual understanding of Benchmark Vocabulary. Students read text closely and use text evidence in their written answers.

Name ______________________________

Writing

Informative/Explanatory Writing: Research a Concept and Write an Essay Use your Main Idea graphic organizer and planning notes to help you research the topic of *courage* or *freedom.* Focus on finding examples from biographies, memoirs, and autobiographies that support your definition of your topic. Then write a one- or two-page essay about the meaning of your chosen word. Your essay should include the definition of *courage* or *freedom* that you developed in the previous lesson, researched supporting facts and details relating to the topic, and your own conclusions about the topic as it relates to your own life. Use a separate sheet of paper or start a new document.

Conventions

Use Strategies to Improve Expression

DIRECTIONS Read the paragraph below and revise it to improve the expression of ideas. Rewrite the paragraph to clarify language and correct grammar, vary sentences, and use a consistent tone and style for informative writing.

Researching the lives of ordinary people can be difficult for several reasons. First of all, it's really hard to find information about people who are not famous. But that doesn't mean that them did not accomplish anything. Or that his lives are not worth writing about. Second of all, not all information is available online. If the person is still living you should interview them if possible. Third of all, you have to make sure that the information you find is true! A responsible writer makes a serious effort to check the accuracy of all information about a person, using credible sources.

____

____

____

____

____

____

____

____

Students write routinely for a range of tasks, purposes, and audiences. Students practice various conventions of standard English.

Name ______________________________

Benchmark Vocabulary

DIRECTIONS Write a sentence using each word.

symmetry consistency precariously

____

____

____

____

____

____

Write in Response to Reading

Crane-man has lived a difficult life and is still able to show great care and concern for Tree-ear. Write a paragraph using text evidence to support this analysis of Crane-man. Write your paragraph below, on a separate sheet of paper, or in a new document.

____

____

____

____

____

____

____

____

____

____

____

Students demonstrate contextual understanding of Benchmark Vocabulary. Students read text closely and use text evidence in their written answers.

Name ____________________

Writing

Argument Writing: Understand Purpose and Structure Focusing on the first two chapters of *A Single Shard*, begin to collect text evidence about Tree-ear and Crane-man's relationship. Remember that eventually you will choose from your collected text evidence to make and support a claim.

- Select and record text evidence about the characters' relationship.
- Use quotation marks to quote the text and note the page number where each piece of text evidence is found.
- Write a question you have about each piece of text evidence.

Use a separate sheet of paper or start a new document.

Conventions

Possessive Pronouns

DIRECTIONS Complete each sentence with the correct possessive pronoun: *mine, yours, his, hers, ours, theirs,* or *whose*.

1. After two months of hard work preparing for the competition, Paul and Maria knew the prize would be ____________.
2. I'm happy with all I've achieved so far, but one day the title of President will be ____________!
3. We've looked everywhere for the missing keys. Perhaps those under the table are ____________?
4. "Is this backpack ____________?" my teacher asked yesterday as I stood up to leave.
5. Megan borrowed my dress for the party, but the shoes she wore were ____________.
6. "____________ is this?" he asked, holding up the sweatshirt.

Students write routinely for a range of tasks, purposes, and audiences. Students practice various conventions of standard English.

Name ______________________________

Borrowed Words

DIRECTIONS Write the English word on the line next to the foreign word that is most like it.

________	**1.** asquutasquash	false
________	**2.** moos	embassy
________	**3.** patata	tomato
________	**4.** magister	squash
________	**5.** agentia	breeze
________	**6.** ambassee	moose
________	**7.** vainilla	diplomacy
________	**8.** zucchino	maestro
________	**9.** fals	sonnet
________	**10.** logistique	potato
________	**11.** sonetto	zucchini
________	**12.** tomate	hickory
________	**13.** pawcohiccora	vanilla
________	**14.** brisa	logistics
________	**15.** diplomatie	agency

Students apply grade-level word analysis skills.

Name ________________________________

Benchmark Vocabulary

DIRECTIONS Write a sentence using each word.

resentful   diligent   insolence

Write in Response to Reading

Reread pages 25, 26, and 36 of *A Single Shard*. Using descriptions, words, thoughts, and actions from the text, explain why Tree-ear feels ashamed in these two scenes and what this tells readers about his character. Write your answer below, on a separate sheet of paper, or in a new document.

Students demonstrate contextual understanding of Benchmark Vocabulary. Students read text closely and use text evidence in their written answers.

Name ____

Character and Plot Development

DIRECTIONS Using evidence from the text, answer the following questions about pages 25–37 of *A Single Shard.*

1. On pages 35 and 36, Crane-man explains to Tree-ear how he lost his cane trying to catch flounder. Why does Tree-ear feel shame in response to this event?

____

____

2. How does Tree-ear react to receiving lunch on pages 33 and 34? What does this response reveal about his character?

____

____

____

3. What details on page 29 suggest that Tree-ear feels nervous about asking Min if he could keep working?

____

____

____

4. Reread pages 26 and 30 where Tree-ear speaks directly to Min. What does Tree-ear's use of the third person when talking to Min reveal about how he views him?

____

____

____

Students analyze and respond to literary or informational text.

Name ______________________________

Writing

Argument Writing: Gather and Analyze Text Evidence You will write one to two paragraphs about Tree-ear and Crane-man's relationship in *A Single Shard*. Your paragraphs should be based on the text evidence you gathered and the analysis and inferences you made. Begin by reading your T-Charts and highlighting the text evidence, analysis, and inference that will most likely give rise to a claim. You do not need to state a claim yet, but you should keep possible claims in mind. Your paragraphs should detail what your findings show about the characters' relationship and touch on ideas that lead in the direction of the claim.

Write your paragraphs on a separate sheet of paper or start a new document. First, state an inference you made. Then list your reasons for making that inference. Include your analysis and the text evidence that supports your inference. Remember to include the page numbers of any quoted text.

Conventions

Ensure Correct Case for Pronouns

DIRECTIONS Circle the mistake in each sentence and write the correct pronoun on the line.

1. Alex and me watched TV last night until after 11 p.m. because the show was so interesting. ________
2. Today's science quiz was really easy for I but it was very difficult for Sam. ________
3. Isabel asked for a souvenir from Mexico, so I bought a handmade purse for them. ________
4. When we visited the farm, we noticed the horse's saddle had a tear in him. ________

Choose the Correct Pronoun

DIRECTIONS Circle the correct pronoun to complete each of the following sentences.

5. This is just the right spot for you and me/I to set up our art display.
6. She and me/I enjoyed a walk together.

Students write routinely for a range of tasks, purposes, and audiences. Students practice various conventions of standard English.

Name ______________________________

Benchmark Vocabulary

DIRECTIONS Write a sentence using each word.

crevices resigned renowned

Write in Response to Reading

Reread the descriptions about Tree-ear on pages 44–46. Use key details from the text to write a brief summary that tells how Tree-ear's skills of "keeping his ears open" and learning "without being taught" are helping him accomplish his goals. Write your answer below, on a separate sheet of paper, or in a new document.

Students demonstrate contextual understanding of Benchmark Vocabulary. Students read text closely and use text evidence in their written answers.

Name ___________________________________

The Hat Man

The first day, when Mr. Hatton had helped out in reading corner, the four-year-olds had yawned and squirmed in response to his soft, slow voice. The second day, when he had sat at the art table, he couldn't think of anything to paint. Volunteering at a nursery school wasn't turning out quite as he'd thought it would. In fact, it was turning out to be as challenging as pulling a rabbit out of a hat.

Today Ms. Chen, the lead teacher, had assigned Mr. Hatton to imaginative play. Feeling glum, he didn't know how he was going to amuse the fidgety four-year-olds. Indeed, he was thinking to himself, *I'm too old to be trying to relate to these little ones* when he spotted a pile of dress-up clothes. It was the hats in that pile that told him that maybe he could accommodate his audience and enjoy himself, too.

Gathering the children around him, he announced excitedly that they would play a mystery guessing game called "What's My Hat?" He would pretend to be someone, and when the children guessed who he was, they could find the right hat and put it on his head.

First, Mr. Hatton said *clip clop, clip clop* and neighed as he marched around the children. All the while he moved his body up and down as if he were galloping on a horse. As he swung an imaginary rope over his head, Helene ran for the cowboy hat. Mr. Hatton bowed low enough for her to place the hat on his head, all the while neighing. Then he removed the hat, twirled around with a flourish to signal he was starting over, and wailed like a fire engine siren. As he did so, he pantomimed pointing a squirting hose at a burning building. This time it was Diego who grabbed the right hat and, with a smile, placed it on Mr. Hatton's head.

The children were engaged, eagerly crowding around him as he made silly sounds and pantomimed clues that drew forth the police officer's cap, the pirate's hat, the queen's crown, the bike rider's helmet, and the construction worker's hard hat. Nobody—not even Mr. Hatton himself—wanted to stop playing when snack time came. In fact, for many days later, Helene was calling Mr. Hatton "Mr. Hat Man," and Mr. Hatton was satisfied with the new hat he was wearing in life.

Students read text closely to determine what the text says.

Name ______________________________

Gather Evidence Underline the sentences that best describe Mr. Hatton's dilemma at the beginning of the story.

Gather Evidence: Extend Your Ideas Review the sentences you underlined. How does this description of Mr. Hatton's feelings relate to the rest of the story? Discuss your ideas with a partner.

____

____

____

Ask Questions Place brackets around the interactions Mr. Hatton has with Ms. Chen, Helene, and Diego. Based on the text, write three questions Ms. Chen, Helene, and Diego might ask Mr. Hatton about his volunteer experiences.

____

____

Ask Questions: Extend Your Ideas Use evidence from the text to write how Mr. Hatton might respond to these questions.

____

____

Make Your Case Do you think Mr. Hatton has changed by the end of story? How? Explain your opinion, citing text evidence in your response.

____

____

____

Make Your Case: Extend Your Ideas Do you think it is important for people to be willing to try on "new hats" throughout their lives? Cite details from the text that support your answer.

____

____

____

Students read text closely to determine what the text says.

Name ______________________________

Writing

Argument Writing: Write a Strong Claim and Introduction After you have collected relevant text evidence from Chapter 4 of *A Single Shard,* write an introduction to your argument that contains a clear claim about Tree-ear and Crane-man's relationship.

In your introduction, provide context about the characters from the story, clearly state the claim, and introduce the main reasons for your claim.

____

____

____

Conventions

Recognizing and Correcting Vague Pronouns

DIRECTIONS Have students underline the vague pronoun in each sentence and rewrite the sentences to correct each one.

1. I was late, so on my way out the door I grabbed an apple and my homework and shoved it in my bag.

____

____

2. The field was full of excitement as they got ready to run the mile.

____

____

3. Alice carefully tipped the extra water out of the pot into the sink, and then put the lid back on it.

____

____

Students write routinely for a range of tasks, purposes, and audiences. Students practice various conventions of standard English.

Name ____________________

Benchmark Vocabulary

DIRECTIONS Write a sentence using each word.

vigilance translucent arduous replicas

Write in Response to Reading

Reread page 69 beginning at the break through the top of page 70. Choose an example of figurative language used in the excerpt and write a paragraph explaining what it means and how it helps set the tone of the scene. Write your answer below, on a separate sheet of paper, or in a new document.

Students demonstrate contextual understanding of Benchmark Vocabulary. Students read text closely and use text evidence in their written answers.

Name ______________________________

Figurative Language

DIRECTIONS Reread the pages noted in each question from pages 49–72 of *A Single Shard.*

1. Reread the first sentence of Chapter 5 on page 49. How does the author set the scene? What tone does this description convey?

____

____

____

2. Reread the last paragraph on page 61 and analyze the description of Kang: "Listening, saying little, his eyes half-closed and a half-smile on his face, Kang looked like nothing so much as a man with a secret." What tone does this description evoke? Would anyone but Tree-ear describe Kang this way at this moment? Explain your answer.

____

____

____

____

3. On page 64, after Crane-man answers Tree-ear's "question-demon," Tree-ear still cannot sleep. The text says, "An image floated out of the darkness into Tree-ear's mind…" What is that image, and where did it really come from?

____

____

____

4. Reread the paragraph on page 72 in which this figurative language appears: "The other potters seemed to slump as one into dejection…" What does this figurative language add to the tone of this paragraph?

____

____

____

Students analyze and respond to literary and informational text.

Name ____________________

Writing

Argument Writing: Support a Claim with Reasons and Evidence Create an outline of your body paragraphs for your critical review about Tree-ear and Crane-man's relationship in *A Single Shard.* Remember to include a minimum of three reasons and an explanation about how the text evidence supports each reason. You may wish to include your introductory paragraph at the top of your outline.

Make sure you support each reason with text evidence, using quotation marks around any direct quotes.

Use a separate sheet of paper. You may also start a new document or continue using the document you created when you wrote your introduction.

Conventions

Possessive Pronouns vs. Possessive Adjectives

DIRECTIONS Circle the possessive word in each sentence. On the line, write whether it is a possessive pronoun or a possessive adjective.

1. "If you finish all your homework, I'll take you to the movies later," my mom said as she left for work this morning. ____________
2. Janie is turning fifteen tomorrow, and Dad bought a chocolate cake for her party. ____________
3. Charlie was working on an art project in the kitchen, so that mess must be his. ____________
4. How many people do you think go to the beach for their vacation? ____________
5. Although we're not sure what the best option is, the choice is ours to make. ____________

Students write routinely for a range of tasks, purposes, and audiences. Students practice various conventions of standard English.

Name ______________________________

Benchmark Vocabulary

DIRECTIONS Write a sentence using each word.

harangued intricate tumultuous

Write in Response to Reading

Reread pages 74–81. Use text evidence to write an explanatory paragraph that describes the conflict Min faces and how it affects his work and attitude. Write your answer below, on a separate sheet of paper, or in a new document.

Students demonstrate contextual understanding of Benchmark Vocabulary. Students read text closely and use text evidence in their written answers.

Name ____

Writing

Argument Writing: Draft a Body Paragraph Look over your claim, introduction, and outline. Make any adjustments that are needed based on new ideas gained during this lesson's reading. Then use your outline to draft the first body paragraph of your critical review about Tree-ear and Crane-man's relationship. Remember to do the following:

- Give one reason and its supporting evidence.
- Use a formal style.
- Write in the third person, avoiding personal opinions.

Use a separate sheet of paper or start a new document.

Conventions

Possessive Pronouns vs. Contractions

DIRECTIONS Circle each mistake and write the correct word on the line. Not every sentence has a mistake, and correct sentences should be marked as Correct.

1. That book on the red table over there is their's. _______
2. If you study hard, you'll definitely pass the test and the prize will be yours! _______
3. How many times must you continue to wear this sweater? It's not yours—it's her's! _______
4. We all laughed as the dog chased it's tail around and around in circles. _______
5. We finally realized that the choice was ours; we didn't need to wait for the teacher to tell us which topic to use. _______
6. You shouldn't have wasted so much time looking for your gloves. You could've just borrowed mine's. _______

Students write routinely for a range of tasks, purposes, and audiences. Students practice various conventions of standard English.

Name ______________________________

Benchmark Vocabulary

DIRECTIONS Write a sentence using each word.

kneaded endeavor defiant

Write in Response to Reading

Reread pages 100–104. Write a paragraph that objectively summarizes how the characters show respect and concern for each other. Write your answer below, on a separate sheet of paper, or in a new document.

Students demonstrate contextual understanding of Benchmark Vocabulary. Students read text closely and use text evidence in their written answers.

Name ________________________

Writing

Argument Writing: Draft Body Paragraphs Use your outline to continue drafting your critical review about Tree-ear and Crane-man's relationship. Write two additional body paragraphs, one for each remaining reason. Use transitional words, phrases, and clauses to show connections among the claim, reasons, and evidence.

Remember to use a logical structure and a formal style. Write your two new paragraphs on a separate sheet of paper or new document, or add to your existing draft.

Conventions

Compound Sentences

DIRECTIONS Read each simple sentence. Then add a conjunction and another independent clause to create a compound sentence.

1. My cat's collar has a bell on it.

____

2. The town was decorated with lights.

____

3. The weather was finally warm enough to swim.

____

4. My science teacher is popular.

____

5. Marie learned to ski when she was four years old.

____

6. It has been raining for two days now.

____

Students write routinely for a range of tasks, purposes, and audiences. Students practice various conventions of standard English.

Name ______________________________

Greek and Latin Roots *spec, mem, ortho, rupt*

DIRECTIONS Match the word with the definition. Use a dictionary, glossary, or thesaurus to confirm your answers.

1. something to remind people of something or someone ____ **a.** orthographical

2. dishonest behavior by those in power ____ **b.** introspection

3. act of looking into one's own thoughts ____ **c.** memo

4. relating to correct spelling ____ **d.** corruption

5. brief written message ____ **e.** memorial

DIRECTIONS Write the word from the Word Bank that best completes each sentence. Use a dictionary, glossary, or thesaurus to confirm your answers.

Word Bank

unorthodox	commemorative	prospective	circumspect
eruption	memorabilia	orthotic	incorruptible
speculative	bankruptcy		

6. After his accident, Brad wore a(n) __________ to support his neck.

7. We thought the politician was __________ and would never abuse his power in any way.

8. The principal did not like the teacher's __________ teaching methods.

9. My teacher met and interviewed all the __________ candidates for the intern job.

10. A good scientist shouldn't draw __________ conclusions.

11. Those __________ stamps were printed to honor Martin Luther King Jr.

12. The company had to declare __________ because it could not pay all of its debts.

13. A volcanic __________ is very dangerous as hot lava, ash, and steam are spewed into the air.

14. The attorney is very cautious and __________ when dealing with a new client.

15. My dad has __________ from the wedding of the British royal couple.

Students apply grade-level word analysis skills.

Name ______________________________

Benchmark Vocabulary

DIRECTIONS Write a sentence using each word.

hospitality trepidation plying impeccable

Write in Response to Reading

Review the narrator's description of Min and Tree-ear's parting on page 109. Use text evidence to write an opinion about why Tree-ear "almost flinched" at Min's touch. Write your answer below, on a separate sheet of paper, or in a new document.

Students demonstrate contextual understanding of Benchmark Vocabulary. Students read text closely and use text evidence in their written answers.

Name ____

Point of View

DIRECTIONS Using evidence from the text, answer the following questions about Chapter 10 from *A Single Shard.*

1. Reread the third paragraph on page 111. How does the narrator's description of Tree-ear starting the fire deepen your understanding of Tree-ear's relationship with Crane-man?

____

____

____

____

2. In the first two paragraphs on page 118, how does the narrator's point of view give readers a vivid picture of Puyo?

____

____

____

____

3. On page 119, why is "*inlaid with chrysanthemums*" in italics? What information is the narrator relating to readers?

____

____

____

____

Students analyze and respond to literary and informational text.

Name ______________________

Argument Writing: Assess Strength of an Argument Assess your own argument for reliability, sufficiency, and accuracy. Identify weak points in your argument, and add additional text evidence to strengthen your argument if needed. Then use your assessment to make revisions to the draft of your critical review about Tree-ear and Crane-man's relationship.

Maintain a formal style in your writing. Use a separate sheet of paper or start a new document.

Complex Sentences Circle *S* (Simple) or *C* (Complex) to describe each sentence. Expand the simple sentences into complex sentences.

1. Since John loves to play soccer, he looks forward to Saturdays when he can spend all day playing with friends. S / C ______________________
2. The first snowfall was early this year. S / C ______________________
____
3. The women walked for hours until their feet were too tired to continue. S / C
____
4. By the time the storm passed, most of the leaves had already blown off the trees. S / C ______________________
5. Henry felt confident that he had gotten a good grade. S / C ______________________
____

Students write routinely for a range of tasks, purposes, and audiences. Students practice various conventions of standard English.

Name ____________________

DIRECTIONS Write a sentence using each word.

incredulous brazen chastened

Write in Response to Reading

Reread the scene involving Tree-ear and the robbers beginning on page 121. Use text evidence to write an explanatory paragraph that tells how Tree-ear shows courage during this conflict. Write your answer below, on a separate sheet of paper, or in a new document.

Students demonstrate contextual understanding of Benchmark Vocabulary. Students read text closely and use text evidence in their written answers.

Name ______________________________________

Writing

Argument Writing: Write a Conclusion Write a conclusion for your critical review about Tree-ear and Crane-man's relationship. Remember to maintain a formal style.

Include the following elements in your conclusion:

- Remind readers of the main claim.
- Summarize the argument without being repetitive.
- Add a final insight to help your reader think more about the argument.

Use a separate sheet of paper, start a new document, or add to an existing document.

Conventions

Correcting Run-On Sentences

DIRECTIONS Correct each run-on sentence on the line provided. If a sentence is complete and does not need corrections, write *correct* on the line.

1. Molly stopped at the grocery store on the way home, she picked up ingredients to make a quick dinner.

____

____

2. The swimmers lined up by the edge of the pool even though the race wasn't starting for another fifteen minutes.

____

____

3. The school invested in new computers, every student would have access to one.

____

____

4. Although comedies are my favorite type of movie, I really like science fiction, too.

____

____

Students write routinely for a range of tasks, purposes, and audiences. Students practice various conventions of standard English.

Name ______________________________

Benchmark Vocabulary

DIRECTIONS Write a sentence using each word.

welter succored assiduous

Write in Response to Reading

Reread the scenes between Tree-ear and Min on pages 142–143 and 146–147. Summarize how Min's character has changed over the course of the story. In what ways has Min's character remained the same? Write your answer below, on a separate sheet of paper, or in a new document.

Students demonstrate contextual understanding of Benchmark Vocabulary. Students read text closely and use text evidence in their written answers.

Name ____________________

Writing

Argument Writing: Write and Apply an Extended Definition Write an argument essay of two to three paragraphs in which you apply the extended definition of *courage* to the four main characters of *A Single Shard* to show that one character is the most courageous. You will make a claim about who is most courageous and cite reasons and evidence to support the claim.

Recall that an argument includes the following:

- An introduction—in this case your extended definition of *courage*
- A clear claim—in this case the character you believe is the most courageous
- Clear reasons and relevant text evidence to support the claim
- A concluding statement or section that reminds readers of the main claim and leaves them with a final insight

Use a separate sheet of paper or start a new document.

Conventions

Correcting Sentence Fragments

DIRECTIONS Underline each sentence fragment. Then correct each fragment by combining or adding information.

1. Slowly came down the road toward the house.

____

2. They made several improvements. In the latest version of the software.

____

3. As the party came to an end. Sam realized he'd lost his phone.

____

4. By the time the movie had finished.

____

Students write routinely for a range of tasks, purposes, and audiences. Students practice various conventions of standard English.

Name ____________________

Benchmark Vocabulary

DIRECTIONS Write a sentence using each word.

recruit grudgingly relinquishes

Write in Response to Reading

Reread pages 46–50 of "No Vacancy" to identify the key details that convey the position of Phillips Exeter Academy on including African American students. Write an informative paragraph in which you summarize their policy. Write your answer below, on a separate sheet of paper, or in a new document.

Students demonstrate contextual understanding of Benchmark Vocabulary. Students read text closely and use text evidence in their written answers.

Name ____________________

Summarize

DIRECTIONS Using evidence from the text, answer the following questions about pages 46–53 from "No Vacancy."

1. Citing evidence from pages 47–49, summarize the conversations between Mrs. Leach and Miss Sparrow. How do these characters help to convey a central idea?

2. Based on Scene One, summarize the differences in how Lewis and Raymond are treated and how these differences contribute to the theme. Cite details in support.

3. Which details from the play suggest that the setting is the 1930s.

4. Summarize the emotions Raymond feels as the play proceeds, and cite the reasons. What does the play's ending reveal about Raymond?

Students analyze and respond to literary and informational text.

Name ______________________________

Writing

Argument Writing: Research a Topic Find credible sources and take notes on how African Americans were treated during the time period in which "No Vacancy" is set. Consider how the concept of freedom can be applied to what you discover as you research and take notes.

Take notes in which you

- Paraphrase and quote text evidence relevant to the topic.
- List author, publisher, and other publication information for each source.
- Consider the idea of freedom and look for ideas about freedom as you research.

Take notes and list your sources on a separate sheet of paper or a new document. Then write a paragraph based on your research below. This paragraph should explain how African Americans were treated during the time period of "No Vacancy."

____

____

____

____

____

____

Conventions

Intensive Pronouns

DIRECTIONS Complete each sentence with an intensive pronoun.

1. The school ____________ was the main reason so many people visited the town.
2. John ____________ wrote the letter to the principal.
3. "How many times have I had to do the shopping ____________?" Mom asked.
4. You ____________ even admitted that you liked to watch that show on TV!
5. Mariana ____________ saved enough money to pay for the entire trip.
6. The actors ____________ built the set and wrote all the stage directions for the school play.

Students write routinely for a range of tasks, purposes, and audiences. Students practice various conventions of standard English.

Name ______________________________

Benchmark Vocabulary

DIRECTIONS Write a sentence using each word.

relinquishes brazen

Write in Response to Reading

Reread pages 60–61 of *A Single Shard* and pages 48–52 of "No Vacancy." How do the people in Tree-ear's village view and treat him, and how do the members of the Phillips Exeter administration view and treat Raymond? Write a paragraph comparing and contrasting the way Tree-ear and Raymond are seen and treated unkindly by others. Write your answer below, on a separate sheet of paper, or in a new document.

Students demonstrate contextual understanding of Benchmark Vocabulary. Students read text closely and use text evidence in their written answers.

Name ______________________________

Writing

Argument Writing: Develop Voice Use the research from print and digital resources that you collected in Lesson 10 as well as text evidence from ”No Vacancy” to write an extended definition of *freedom* that reflects Raymond's point of view.

Write one to two pages in which you do the following:

- Give a definition of *freedom* as it applies to Raymond.
- Develop your definition to reflect Raymond's point of view using facts from your research and text evidence from "No Vacancy."
- Use a writing voice that shows Raymond's personality.

Use a separate sheet of paper or start a new document.

Conventions

Common Problems with Intensive Pronouns

DIRECTIONS Cross off any incorrect intensive pronouns. If a correction is needed, write the correct intensive pronoun on the line.

1. The school herself was the most interesting building in the town.

   ____

2. I myself was willing to stay up all night and help out if necessary.

   ____

3. Why don't they themself clean up the mess?

   ____

4. We ourself knew that the only way to pass the test was to study the entire book.

   ____

5. She herself admitted to entering the building after hours.

   ____

6. How many times can he hisself continue to waste all that money?

   ____

Students write routinely for a range of tasks, purposes, and audiences. Students practice various conventions of standard English.

Name ______________________________

Greek and Latin Suffixes *-en, -age, -ment, -ic, -ous, -ation*

DIRECTIONS Complete the chart by adding the suffix, suffix meaning, part of speech, and meaning for each word.

	Suffix	Suffix Meaning	Part of Speech	Word Meaning
1. mischievous				
2. imagination				
3. employment				
4. leaden				
5. automatic				
6. spoilage				

DIRECTIONS Read the sentences and use your understanding of the meanings of Greek and Latin suffixes and the base words to define the underlined words.

7. Much to the students' bewilderment, the teachers strolled the halls singing blues songs.

____

8. Joan was ecstatic to learn that her dog won second prize at the dog show.

____

9. Avi shows great determination to succeed when faced with a new challenge.

____

10. She could not believe the shrinkage of her sweater after she washed it.

____

11. Kira turned ashen when asked whether she remembered to turn in her report.

____

12. Imagine the deprivation of having no access to clean water after a natural disaster.

____

Students apply grade-level word analysis skills.

Name ____________________

Benchmark Vocabulary

DIRECTIONS Write a sentence using each word.

diplomacy agitators reconciliation

Write in Response to Reading

Reread the end-of-book biography in *Nelson Mandela.* Mandela was very involved in South African politics over the course of his lifetime. Write one paragraph summarizing Mandela's political roles and activities in South Africa. Be sure to include a central idea and key details. Write your answer below, on a separate sheet of paper, or in a new document.

Students demonstrate contextual understanding of Benchmark Vocabulary. Students read text closely and use text evidence in their written answers.

Name ______________________________

Determine the Central Idea

DIRECTIONS Using evidence from the text, respond to the following items about *Nelson Mandela.*

1. How did Mandela's childhood influence his role in ending apartheid?

2. On pages 27–29, the author indicates that while Nelson Mandela was in prison, protests continued and world nations joined in the protest against apartheid and won. Using text details, write a summary about the state of Africa when Nelson Mandela got out of prison.

3. Use text details to summarize Nelson Mandela's point of view on whether South Africans who had been oppressed for so long should punish their oppressors under Mandela's presidency.

Students analyze and respond to literary and informational text.

Name ____________________

Writing

Argument Writing: Checking for Bias The theme of a work is the overall message that the writer is trying to convey. Gather evidence about the theme of *Nelson Mandela* and use it to develop a claim. Support your claim with clear reasons and relevant evidence in a two- to three-page argument essay.

In your argument, remember to:

- Introduce the topic and state a claim about the theme of the text.
- Support the claim with clear reasons and text evidence.
- Provide a concluding statement or section.
- Use a formal style and eliminate any bias from your argument.

Use a separate sheet of paper or start a new document.

Conventions

Punctuating Titles of Works

DIRECTIONS Underline or add quotation marks to the titles of works in the sentences below.

1. The main characters in the book A Long Way Home were lost in the woods for several weeks.
2. Our science teacher assigned the chapter Animal Adaptations from the book The World of Science for homework.
3. My favorite poem is If by Rudyard Kipling, who also wrote the novel The Jungle Book.
4. My sister and I have been reading A Tale of Two Cities out loud for the past week.
5. I can't wait to read the new article called Top 10 Best Videogames.

Students write routinely for a range of tasks, purposes, and audiences. Students practice various conventions of standard English.

Name ______________________________

Benchmark Vocabulary

DIRECTIONS Write a sentence using each word.

negotiations sanctions eradication

Write in Response to Reading

Reread pages 56–57. Who carries the primary responsibility for bringing about social and political change, the people or the leaders? Write a paragraph stating your argument and using evidence from the text to support your response. Write your answer below, on a separate sheet of paper, or in a new document.

Students demonstrate contextual understanding of Benchmark Vocabulary. Students read text closely and use text evidence in their written answers.

Name ______________________________________

Eulogy for Dr. Dorothy Height by President Barack Obama

Below is an excerpt from a eulogy that President Barack Obama delivered in honor of educator and social activist Dr. Dorothy Height on April 29, 2010, praising her life and describing it as "a life that lifted other lives; a life that changed this country for the better over the course of nearly one century here on Earth."

Progress came from the collective effort of multiple generations of Americans. From preachers and lawyers, and thinkers and doers, men and women like Dr. Height, who took it upon themselves—often at great risk—to change this country for the better…. Well, Dr. Dorothy Height deserves a place in this pantheon. She, too, deserves a place in our history books. She, too, deserves a place of honor in America's memory.

Look at her body of work. Desegregating the YWCA. Laying the groundwork for integration on Wednesdays in Mississippi. Lending pigs to poor farmers as a sustainable source of income. Strategizing with civil rights leaders, holding her own, the only woman in the room, Queen Esther to this Moses Generation—even as she led the National Council of Negro Women with vision and energy—with vision and energy, vision and class.

But we remember her not solely for all she did during the civil rights movement. We remember her for all she did over a lifetime, behind the scenes, to broaden the movement's reach. To shine a light on stable families and tight-knit communities. To make us see the drive for civil rights and women's rights not as a separate struggle, but as part of a larger movement to secure the rights of all humanity, regardless of gender, regardless of race, regardless of ethnicity.

It's an unambiguous record of righteous work, worthy of remembrance, worthy of recognition. And yet, one of the ironies is, is that year after year, decade in, decade out, Dr. Height went about her work quietly, without fanfare, without self-promotion. She never cared about who got the credit. She didn't need to see her picture in the papers. She understood that the movement gathered strength from the bottom up, those unheralded men and women who don't always make it into the history books but who steadily insisted on their dignity, on their manhood and womanhood. She wasn't interested in credit. What she cared about was the cause. The cause of justice. The cause of equality. The cause of opportunity.

Students read text closely to determine what the text says.

Name ______________________________

Gather Evidence Underline the words or phrases that describe how Dr. Height approached her work. Next, circle the words that describe the work itself.

Gather Evidence: Extend Your Ideas Review the text details you underlined and circled. Why do you think the author includes these details? What is the author's point of view?

____

____

Ask Questions Write three questions you have about the civil rights movement based on Dr. Height's contribution to it. Where can you find answers to your questions?

____

____

Ask Questions: Extend Your Ideas Write what you imagine Dr. Height's response would be if she were asked to name her most important contribution to the advancement of civil rights, and then write why you think this.

____

____

Make Your Case Bracket portions of text that tell about the causes that were important to Dr. Height. In what ways are these causes relevant to people today? Write your ideas below.

____

____

____

Make Your Case: Extend Your Ideas Which of the causes you bracketed do you think is most important for our nation to work to resolve? Discuss your point of view with a partner and use details in the text to support your response.

____

____

____

Students read text closely to determine what the text says.

Name ______________________________

Writing

Argument Writing: Analyze Author's Purpose Gather evidence in support of a claim about the purpose of Nelson Mandela's speech "Our March to Freedom Is Irreversible." Write one to two pages to support your claim with reasons and evidence. Make sure that you clearly state a claim about the purpose of the speech, support your claim with reasons and evidence, and use transitions to connect reasons with text evidence. Conclude your essay with a restatement of your claim. Use a separate sheet of paper or start a new document.

Conventions

Punctuating Direct Address

DIRECTIONS Add commas where needed to punctuate the direct addresses that occur in the sentences below. If the sentence is correct, write "no change."

1. Ladies and gentlemen I present to you the amazing Houdini!

   ____

2. Barack Obama was the president after George Bush.

   ____

3. I want to show that it is possible my fellow countrymen to make a lasting change.

   ____

4. Members of the board I appeal to you.

   ____

5. Nelson Mandela worked tirelessly for equal rights.

   ____

6. Students we're excited to introduce our next speaker.

   ____

Students write routinely for a range of tasks, purposes, and audiences. Students practice various conventions of standard English.

Name ______________________________

Benchmark Vocabulary

DIRECTIONS Write a sentence using each word.

sanctions diplomacy

____

____

____

____

____

____

Write in Response to Reading

Reread the biography on pages 36–37 in *Nelson Mandela* and pages 56–57 of "Our March to Freedom Is Irreversible." How does Mandela prove to be a leader for the cause against apartheid? Write an informative summary paragraph using details from both texts to support your answer. Write your answer below, on a separate sheet of paper, or in a new document.

____

____

____

____

____

____

____

____

____

____

Students demonstrate contextual understanding of Benchmark Vocabulary. Students read text closely and use text evidence in their written answers.

Name ______________________________

Writing

Argument Writing: Gather and Analyze Evidence Gather evidence about how each character in *A Single Shard* impacts Tree-ear's life, and analyze the evidence to identify which person had the most impact on the kind of person Tree-ear becomes.

In your argument, remember to:

- Collect text evidence about each character's impact on Tree-ear.
- Analyze the text evidence.
- Highlight the text evidence that is most likely to give rise to a claim.
- Draw a conclusion about which character had the greatest impact on Tree-ear.
- Write one to two paragraphs in which you state which character impacted Tree-ear the most, based on your text evidence, and give the reasons you came to this conclusion.

Use a separate sheet of paper or start a new document.

Conventions

Punctuating Quotes

DIRECTIONS Punctuate the following quotes correctly.

1. Our struggle has reached a decisive moment said Nelson Mandela.

2. Martin Luther King Jr. said Free at last! Free at last! Thank God Almighty, we are free at last!

3. Four score and seven years ago our fathers brought forth on this continent, a new nation, conceived in Liberty, and dedicated to the proposition that all men are created equal Abraham Lincoln said at Gettysburg.

4. And so, my fellow Americans John F. Kennedy said ask not what your country can do for you; ask what you can do for your country.

Students write routinely for a range of tasks, purposes, and audiences. Students practice various conventions of standard English.

Name ______________________

Benchmark Vocabulary

DIRECTIONS Write a sentence using each word.

consistency reconciliation

____

____

____

____

Write in Response to Reading

Reread pages 18–19 of *A Single Shard* and page 8 of *Nelson Mandela*. What do the excerpts have in common? Use text evidence to write an informative paragraph that compares and contrasts how each character displays courage through his response to events. Write your answer below, on a separate sheet of paper, or in a new document.

____

____

____

____

____

____

____

____

____

____

____

____

Students demonstrate contextual understanding of Benchmark Vocabulary. Students read text closely and use text evidence in their written answers.

Name ______________________________

Compare and Contrast

DIRECTIONS Using evidence from the texts, respond to the following items about traits Tree-ear and Nelson Mandela show in *A Single Shard* and *Nelson Mandela.*

1. One trait that Tree-ear and Nelson Mandela share is empathy for others. Give two examples from each text that illustrate this trait.

2. Another common character trait between Tree-ear and Nelson Mandela is respect for others. Give two examples from each text that illustrate this trait.

3. A third common character trait between Tree-ear and Nelson Mandela is honor. Give two examples from each text that illustrate how the author develops this trait.

Students analyze and respond to literary and informational text.

Name ______________________________

Writing

Argument Writing: Organize Reasons and Evidence to Support a Claim Write a draft of your critical review. Drafts should include an introductory paragraph that makes a claim, body paragraphs that include clear reasons and relevant text evidence, and a conclusion that follows from the argument presented. Use a separate sheet of paper or start a new document.

Conventions

Use Standard English

DIRECTIONS Read the following nonstandard language and write sentences using the standard form of each word or expression.

woulda	alot	irregardless	could of	gonna

1.
2.
3.
4.
5.

Students write routinely for a range of tasks, purposes, and audiences. Students practice various conventions of standard English.

Name ______________________________

Benchmark Vocabulary

DIRECTIONS Write a sentence using each word.

compel prosper penalty

____
____
____
____
____
____

Write in Response to Reading

Reread the final paragraph on page 59 of "I am Tired of Talk That Comes to Nothing." Evaluate the effectiveness of the paragraph. Was it convincing? Why or why not? Write a paragraph expressing your opinion about the persuasiveness of the conclusion of the speech. Write your answer below, on a separate sheet of paper, or in a new document.

____
____
____
____
____
____
____
____
____
____

Students demonstrate contextual understanding of Benchmark Vocabulary. Students read text closely and use text evidence in their written answers.

Name ______________________________

Writing

Argument Writing: Use Transitions to Clarify Relationships Revise your critical review draft. Remember the writing prompt: *The author of* A Single Shard *limits the number of characters that impact Tree-Ear's life. Which character—Crane-man, Min, or Min's wife—has the most impact on the type of person Tree-Ear becomes?*

As you revise, be sure to add transitional words, phrases, and clauses to clarify connections between your claim, reasons, and evidence. Use a formal style, including precise language. Evaluate the effectiveness of reasons and evidence and add more evidence if needed.

Use a separate sheet of paper or start a new document.

Conventions

Spell Correctly

DIRECTIONS Cross off the misspelled words in the following sentences. Write the correct spelling on the line.

1. That nature fotographer is incredibly talented. ______________
2. Alex bought fresh vegtables to cut up for the soup. ______________
3. Marie's gidence counselor requested to see her after school. ______________
4. It was difficult to remember my new class skedule. ______________
5. I was happy because Mom said my cake was egcelent! ______________
6. The solution to the problem was intristing; I never would have figured it out on my own. ______________

Students write routinely for a range of tasks, purposes, and audiences. Students practice various conventions of standard English.

Name ______________________________

Word Relationships: Analogies

DIRECTIONS Write the type of analogy—part/whole, item/category, or cause/effect—for each word pair.

1. petal : flower ____________________
2. volleyball : sport ____________________
3. tires : auto ____________________
4. lake : body of water ____________________
5. practice : mastery ____________________

DIRECTIONS Write the word choice that completes each analogy. Then write what type—part/whole, item/category, or cause/effect—the analogy is.

6. shell : egg :: peel : ________________ ________________

   banana   open   seed

7. chair: furniture :: train : ________________ ________________

   tracks   transportation   station

8. clouds : rain :: traffic : ________________ ________________

   delays   highways   cars

9. nickel: coin :: Mars : ________________ ________________

   Earth   planet   space

10. humor : laugh :: tragedy : ________________ ________________

    smile   cry   emotion

11. name : person :: title : ________________ ________________

    call   words   book

DIRECTIONS Fill in the blank to complete the second part of each analogy. Some analogies can have multiple correct answers.

12. shirt : clothing :: dog : ________________
13. noodles : soup :: lettuce : ________________
14. elbow : arm :: toe : ________________
15. horse : herbivore :: tiger : ________________
16. fire : burn :: blizzard : ________________

Students apply grade-level word analysis skills.

Name ______________________________

Benchmark Vocabulary

DIRECTIONS Write a sentence using each word.

diligent vigilance

____

____

____

____

____

____

Write in Response to Reading

Reread *A Single Shard* pages 146–148 and *Nelson Mandela* pages 29–34. What events in each text show the accomplishment of goals, achieved through overcoming adversity? Write two paragraphs comparing and contrasting the texts' approach to this topic. Write your answer below, on a separate sheet of paper, or in a new document.

____

____

____

____

____

____

____

____

____

Students demonstrate contextual understanding of Benchmark Vocabulary. Students read text closely and use text evidence in their written answers.

Name ______________________________

Writing

Argument Writing: Cite Direct Quotes Edit and proofread your revised draft of your critical review. Edit and proofread your draft for correct pronoun usage, correct spelling of difficult words, and correct punctuation within quotes. Use a separate sheet of paper or start a new document.

Conventions

Frequently Confused Words

DIRECTIONS Correct the underlined word in each of the following sentences. Write the correct word on the line.

1. The music had a calming <u>affect</u> on the students taking the test. ______________
2. We all know that Washington, D.C., is the <u>capitol</u> of the United States. ______________
3. Draw a line <u>thorough</u> the center of the circle to divide it in half. ______________
4. My cousins always do <u>they're</u> shopping together around the holidays. ______________
5. Meg secured the money in her purse so she wouldn't <u>loose</u> it. ______________
6. Ted won't eat meat on <u>principal</u>; he cares too much about animals. ______________

Students write routinely for a range of tasks, purposes, and audiences. Students practice various conventions of standard English.

Name ______________________________

Benchmark Vocabulary

DIRECTIONS Write a sentence using each word.

tumultuous endeavor negotiations

Write in Response to Reading

Reread the final paragraph of "Our March to Freedom Is Irreversible" and the final paragraph of "I Am Tired of Talk That Comes to Nothing." Write two paragraphs comparing and contrasting the conclusions of these speeches. Then discuss how the details in these paragraphs convey the central idea of each text. Write your answer below, on a separate sheet of paper, or in a new document.

Students demonstrate contextual understanding of Benchmark Vocabulary. Students read text closely and use text evidence in their written answers.

Name ______________________________

Compare and Contrast Central Ideas

DIRECTIONS Using evidence from the texts, respond to the following questions about *A Single Shard, Nelson Mandela,* "No Vacancy," "Our March to Freedom is Irreversible," and "I Am Tired of Talk That Comes to Nothing."

1. One central idea of "I Am Tired of Talk That Comes to Nothing" and "No Vacancy" is that people cannot deny the rights of others based on race, culture, or ethnicity. Identify key details in each text that develop this central idea.

____
____
____
____
____

2. One central idea of *Nelson Mandela* and "Our March to Freedom Is Irreversible" is that people must learn to live together in harmony. Identify key details in each text that develop this central idea.

____
____
____
____
____

3. How do the literary genres of *A Single Shard* and "No Vacancy" influence the types of details the authors include to develop central ideas?

____
____
____
____
____
____

Students analyze and respond to literary and informational text.

Name ____________________

Argument Writing: Publish and Present Plan with your group and then engage in a class debate.

Your group will need to prepare an opening argument that states the group's main claim and supports it with reasons and evidence. Your group should have prepared anticipated counterarguments and the group's responses to these counterarguments. Finally, your group should prepare a closing statement, in which the group summarizes its main points. Make sure that each person in your group has a chance to speak in the debate. Write your plan on a separate sheet of paper or start a new document.

Use Strategies to Improve Expression

DIRECTIONS Improve the sentences using descriptive language. Write your revised sentences on the lines.

1. We sat on the beach and watched the sunset.

____

____

2. Sharon raked the leaves, but overnight more fell.

____

____

3. The dog drank his water.

____

____

4. The soup was very hot, so I burned my tongue.

____

____

Students write routinely for a range of tasks, purposes, and audiences. Students practice various conventions of standard English.

Name ______________________________

Benchmark Vocabulary

DIRECTIONS Write a sentence using each word.

launch gadget motivate passion

____

____

____

____

____

____

Write in Response to Reading

Reread pages 6–11. Write a one-paragraph summary of Steve Jobs's early years, from childhood through college. Use details from the text in your paragraph. Write your paragraph below, on a separate sheet of paper, or in a new document.

____

____

____

____

____

____

____

____

____

____

____

Students demonstrate contextual understanding of Benchmark Vocabulary. Students read text closely and use text evidence in their written answers.

Name ______________________

Author's Purpose

DIRECTIONS Using evidence from the text, answer the following questions about *Steve Jobs.*

1. What do you learn about how the "new product" is being launched on page 4?

2. Why do you think the author does not explain what the new product is right away?

3. How does the author introduce Steve Wozniak and develop Jobs and Wozniak's friendship?

4. How does the description of Wozniak show that he is a key individual in the biography of Jobs?

Students analyze and respond to literary and informational text.

Name ______________________________

Writing

Argument Writing: Purpose and Structure of an Argument You will be using evidence from pages 4–11 of *Steve Jobs* to support the author's claim that "Jobs was always an independent thinker." Choose relevant evidence from the text to support this claim. Blend the evidence with strong, logical reasons that explain why the claim is true. As you select evidence, consider these questions:

- What does the phrase "independent thinker" mean?
- How does the phrase relate to Jobs, from his youth all the way through his adult life?
- Which examples from the selection best support this view of Steve Jobs?

Write your argument below or on a separate sheet of paper.

____

____

____

____

Conventions

Use Singular and Plural Pronouns

DIRECTIONS Correct the pronoun errors in the sentences below. Then write one new sentence using a singular or plural pronoun that agrees in number with its antecedent.

1. Kira and Michael worked in the computer lab because she had an assignment to complete.

   ____

   ____

2. Mr. Conway offered to help both students, who gratefully thanked them.

   ____

   ____

3. ______________________________

   ____

Students write routinely for a range of tasks, purposes, and audiences. Students practice various conventions of standard English.

Name ______________________________

Greek and Latin Roots *ques, scrib, cogn, therm*

DIRECTIONS Write the meaning of each root and give an example of a word that includes that root.

1. ques: ____________
2. scrib: ____________
3. cogn: ____________
4. therm: ____________

DIRECTIONS Match the definition with the word. Write the word on the line.

1. not certain or in doubt ____________
2. one who writes messily ____________
3. act of knowing ____________
4. relating to heat ____________
5. suggest a treatment ____________
6. knowledge of a future event ____________

a. scribbler
b. cognition
c. thermal
d. questionable
e. precognition
f. prescribe

Word Bank

transcribe	incognito	questioning	thermograph
subscription	recognizably	question	thermic

DIRECTIONS Choose a word from the Word Bank to complete each sentence. Not every word will be used.

1. Mateo's raised eyebrows and ____________ look during the board game made me pull out a dictionary.
2. A ____________ is an instrument that records the temperature that it measures.
3. We all could see that Myra was ____________ excited about filling in as news anchor.
4. No one noticed Shelly, who came ____________ to the party.
5. After the lecture, I will ____________ my handwritten notes from my notebook into my notes file on my computer.

Students apply grade-level word analysis skills.

Name ____________________

Benchmark Vocabulary

DIRECTIONS Write a sentence using the word.

ambitions

____

____

Write in Response to Reading

Reread the sidebars and look at the photos on pages 14–21. Which factors contributed to Steve Jobs's success? Use details from the text and visual features and photos in your paragraph. Write your paragraph below, on a separate sheet of paper, or in a new document.

____

____

____

____

____

____

____

____

____

____

____

____

____

Students demonstrate contextual understanding of Benchmark Vocabulary. Students read text closely and use text evidence in their written answers.

Name ____________________

Text and Visual Features

DIRECTIONS Using evidence from the text, answer the following questions about *Steve Jobs*.

1. The subheading on page 19 refers to the "insanely great" Macintosh. Why was the subheading written this way? Was the author's purpose effective?

2. Turn to page 21. What is the author's purpose for including the photo and caption of Bill Gates?

3. Which of the text or visual features added by the author gives readers a more personal view of Jobs?

Students analyze and respond to literary and informational text.

Name ______________________________

Writing

Argument Writing: Express a Point of View You will be using evidence from *Steve Jobs* to make and support a claim about how the author indicates a specific point of view about Jobs. Review the pages you have read in the text so far. Use evidence from the text to state, support, and develop a claim.

As you review the text, consider

- how the author describes the personality and career of Steve Jobs.
- words the author uses to convey his point of view about Jobs.
- facts, details, and quotations from the selection that can serve as evidence supporting your claim.

Write your argument below, on a separate sheet of paper, or in a new document.

____

____

____

Conventions

Eliminate Pronoun-Antecedent Ambiguity

DIRECTIONS Circle the unclear pronoun. Rewrite the sentences below so that it is clear to whom or what the pronoun refers.

1. Ben traveled with his puppy to Cape Cod on the bus, but it turned out to be a problem.

____

____

2. The dog kept barking until the driver and another boy became annoyed with him.

____

____

3. Ben offered an apology and his headphones to the boy but then took them back during the ride.

____

____

4. The other boy and Ben started to chat, and he invited him to visit his home in the city.

____

Students write routinely for a range of tasks, purposes, and audiences. Students practice various conventions of standard English.

Name ________________________________

Benchmark Vocabulary

DIRECTIONS Write a sentence using each word.

revenge accessible confident

____

____

____

____

____

____

Write in Response to Reading

Reread the following sidebars that highlight people other than Jobs: George Lucas, page 24 and Jonathan Ive, page 31. Write an opinion paragraph that explains which of these individuals played the most significant role in Jobs's career. Write your paragraph below, on a separate sheet of paper, or in a new document.

____

____

____

____

____

____

____

Students demonstrate contextual understanding of Benchmark Vocabulary. Students read text closely and use text evidence in their written answers.

Name ______________________________ **Sleuth Passage**

Getting Comfortable

"Here we are," Amari's dad said as the car came slowly to a halt at the main entrance to the Sunnydale long-term care facility.

Fidgeting with his seat belt, Amari sighed slowly. "I don't want to go in, Dad, and I won't know the first thing to say to the residents," he whined. "What if I can't find anything to do?" he added, closing the door just a little too hard.

When his dad pulled away, Amari walked reluctantly into what everyone at Madison Middle School called the "nursing home" and asked for Ms. James, the volunteer coordinator. Before a minute had passed, she stood in front of him. A tall woman with twinkling eyes, she extended a welcoming hand to Amari. Beside her was a slim, elderly gentleman whom she introduced as Ernesto Acevedo. "Amari," she said, "Ernesto has requested a little company. He'll show you to the activities room where the two of you can get comfortable and chat."

Why, oh why, did I sign up for community service? Amari asked himself as they headed down the hall without exchanging a single word.

When they reached the activities room, Ernesto headed straight for the sofa. Amari followed, watching mutely during the seemingly endless period it took Ernesto to position his walker and then situate himself comfortably on the cushion. Ernesto beckoned Amari to take a seat beside him. Amari hesitated, inhaling slowly, his eyes nervously darting around his surroundings. After several awkward moments of silence, Ernesto reached into his pocket. "Here's what I need," Ernesto announced. Amari steeled himself for viewing pictures of Ernesto's beautiful grandchildren or lost wife (and what could he possibly say to that?), so he was surprised when Ernesto pulled out a shiny black smartphone.

"You see," Ernesto continued as he opened up an app, "I'm just not any good with this slingshot game, and I still don't understand the difference between black, white, green, and red."

Amari glanced at the smartphone and then nodded his head in excitement. He knew the game that Ernesto wanted help with. "Don't worry, Mr. Acevedo," Amari explained as he eagerly reached over to tap the screen. "I can definitely take you up to level six in no time flat!"

When Amari's dad picked him up an hour later, Amari grinned as he slid into the front seat. "Next week can I stay here a little longer?" he asked.

Students read text closely to determine what the text says.

Name ______________________________

Gather Evidence On page 318, underline information that tells what Amari was dreading about his visit to Sunnydale and with Ernesto.

Gather Evidence: Extend Your Ideas What assumption did Amari make that led him to dread his time at Sunnydale and with Ernesto?

____

____

Ask Questions What question could the reader ask Amari about his request to stay longer on his next visit to Sunnydale?

____

____

Ask Questions: Extend Your Ideas Scan the text on page 318, and circle any details that might suggest an answer to your question. Then use that circled text to write another question.

____

____

Make Your Case Put brackets around details that show what Amari and Ernesto have in common. Write them below.

____

____

Make Your Case: Extend Your Ideas If you were Amari, what items would you bring to a second visit with Ernesto? Write them below and explain why they would be useful or fun.

____

____

____

____

Students read text closely to determine what the text says.

Name ____

Writing

Argument Writing: Gather and Analyze Text Evidence Use evidence from the text to determine a quality particularly critical to the success of an entrepreneur. Gather additional evidence from your reading of *Steve Jobs* and analyze the evidence. Write several paragraphs that summarize this data and state your findings. Write your paragraphs on a separate sheet of paper or start a new document.

Conventions

Ensure Proper Case for Pronouns

DIRECTIONS Complete the sentences below by writing the pronoun in the proper case to replace the underlined word.

1. My notes on the subject of technology are useful, but I wish I understood ______ a bit better.
2. If I show you my outline, would you show me ______?
3. The other students are waiting for these reports. Remember, we're going to have to explain our findings to ______.
4. Alicia usually makes helpful comments so we could read our findings to ______ later today.
5. The one with the red cover is his book, and the one with the blue cover is ______.

Students write routinely for a range of tasks, purposes, and audiences. Students practice various conventions of standard English.

Name ________________________________

Benchmark Vocabulary

DIRECTIONS Write a sentence using each word.

quest perfection authority

____

____

____

____

____

____

Write in Response to Reading

Reread pages 36–39 in *Steve Jobs*, paying attention to key details. Use the key details to write a one-paragraph summary of the information on these pages. Write your paragraph below, on a separate sheet of paper, or in a new document.

____

____

____

____

____

____

____

____

____

____

____

Students demonstrate contextual understanding of Benchmark Vocabulary. Students read text closely and use text evidence in their written answers.

Name ____________________

Writing

Argument Writing: Generate a Claim Review the evidence and findings you collected in the previous lesson and determine your claim on which quality is especially important to the success of an entrepreneur. Recall that an entrepreneur is a person who owns and operates a business and usually takes financial risks in order to succeed. Use the evidence you collected in *Steve Jobs* as a starting point for your claim. Write a paragraph in which you state your claim and provide relevant reasons to support the claim. Write your paragraph on a separate sheet of paper or start a new document.

Conventions

Ensure Proper Case for Pronouns

DIRECTIONS Choose the correct subjective, objective, or possessive pronoun from the words in parentheses. Then write the correct pronoun on the line.

1. Paul is one of the most serious science students, and (he/they) often completes projects for extra credit.

   ____

2. Emily and Rita were absent from class today so I offered to give (her/them) my notes.

   ____

3. A science fiction movie was aired on several stations last night, but I didn't see (it's/its) appeal.

   ____

4. Mei Mei and I watched a nature show about wildlife instead, and (we/us) really enjoyed the topic.

   ____

Students write routinely for a range of tasks, purposes, and audiences. Students practice various conventions of standard English.

Name ______________________________

Benchmark Vocabulary

DIRECTIONS Write a sentence using each word.

mourned perspiration

Write in Response to Reading

Reread pages 42–43. Write one paragraph arguing whether you have what it takes to be an entrepreneur. Use details from the text in your paragraph. Write your paragraph below, on a separate sheet of paper, or in a new document.

Students demonstrate contextual understanding of Benchmark Vocabulary. Students read text closely and use text evidence in their written answers.

Name ______________________________

Trace an Argument

DIRECTIONS Using evidence from the text, answer the following questions about *Steve Jobs*.

1. What claim does the author make about Jobs in the section called "Visionary leader" on page 40?

____
____
____
____

2. Explain how the text supports the claim in "Visionary leader." Give at least one example.

____
____
____
____
____
____

3. On pages 42–43, the author advises readers on how to be an entrepreneur. Based on what you've read in *Steve Jobs*, what can you add to his advice? Support your answer with details from the text.

____
____
____
____
____
____

Students analyze and respond to literary and informational text.

Name ________________________________

Writing

Argument Writing: Support a Claim with Reasons and Evidence Create an outline for the three paragraphs that will make up the body of your argument writing about the most important quality of an entrepreneur. Use an outline format to organize the topics and subtopics of your body paragraphs.

As you prepare to write your outline, consider:

- Which of my reasons is most important? Which reasons should I develop next?
- Which pieces of evidence directly support each of these reasons?
- Which details and examples illustrate the supporting reasons?

Write your outline on a separate sheet of paper or start a new document.

Conventions

Ensure Compound Subject-Verb Agreement

DIRECTIONS Choose the verb form that correctly completes the sentence.

1. Running and swimming (is / are) both excellent forms of exercise for aerobic conditioning.
2. On the other hand, neither video games nor television viewing (burn / burns) many calories.
3. Friends and family often (work / works) together to get physically fit.
4. Either an exercise class or a team sport (inspire / inspires) many people to work out regularly.

Students write routinely for a range of tasks, purposes, and audiences. Students practice various conventions of standard English.

Name ______________________________

Benchmark Vocabulary

DIRECTIONS Write a sentence using each word.

benefits distraction

____

____

____

____

Write in Response to Reading

Look at the bar graph on page 12. Select two of the feelings that smartphone owners have about their devices and explain why you think they have each type of feeling. Use the information you read in this section to support your opinion.

____

____

____

____

____

____

____

____

____

____

____

____

____

Students demonstrate contextual understanding of Benchmark Vocabulary. Students read text closely and use text evidence in their written answers.

Name ______________________________

Writing

Argument Writing: Clarify Relationships Among Claim, Reasons, and Evidence Review the outline you wrote for an argument essay about the most critical quality of an entrepreneur. Write a first body paragraph based on the outline that introduces and develops a reason in support of your claim using evidence. Write your response on a separate sheet of paper or start a new document.

Conventions

Use Correlative Conjunctions

DIRECTIONS Rewrite the sentences below, choosing the appropriate correlative conjunction from the pair in parentheses. Then write two new sentences using compound subjects, compound objects, or compound predicates set off by correlative conjunctions.

1. Both sculpture (and / or) painting will be exhibited in the new art museum.
2. Observing (either / neither) working artists (and / or) great masterpieces can teach us about art.
3. ______________________________
   ____
4. ______________________________
   ____

Students write routinely for a range of tasks, purposes, and audiences. Students practice various conventions of standard English.

Name ______________________________

Figurative Language

Word Bank

chirp	cute kitty cat	whoosh	bottomless pit	piles of e-mail
tick	working 24/7	words of wisdom	Dwayne's Deli and Diner	

DIRECTIONS Complete the chart identifying words and phrases in the Word Bank as examples of alliteration, onomatopoeia, and hyperbole. Write each word or phrase in the correct column.

Alliteration: repeats consonant sounds at beginning of words	Onomatopoeia: imitates the sound it represents	Hyperbole: exaggerates actions or events
1. ______________	4. ______________	7. ______________
2. ______________	5. ______________	8. ______________
3. ______________	6. ______________	9. ______________

DIRECTIONS Each item is an example of alliteration, onomatopoeia, or hyperbole. Write on the line the figure of speech used in the sentence.

10. He can run faster than a racehorse! ______________

11. The snake hissed at the approaching mongoose. ______________

12. I selected a sprig of sage, smelled it, and sighed. ______________

13. I could eat ten pounds of spaghetti right now. ______________

DIRECTIONS Write your own example of alliteration, onomatopoeia, and hyperbole using the prompts.

14. hyperbole: Tell how long it would take to do a chore.

____

15. onomatopoeia: Write a sentence about what you might hear in or near your home.

____

16. alliteration: Write a news headline about a school achievement.

____

Students apply grade-level word analysis skills.

Name ____________________

Benchmark Vocabulary

DIRECTIONS Write a sentence using each word.

illegally independent

Write in Response to Reading

Reread pages 20–25. Write a paragraph in which you make an argument for whether technology improves or interferes with family life. Write your answer on the lines below and explain your reasoning. Use text evidence in your answer.

Students demonstrate contextual understanding of Benchmark Vocabulary. Students read text closely and use text evidence in their written answers.

Name ____________________

Writing

Argument Writing: Maintain a Formal Style Review your outline and earlier paragraphs. Write the remaining two paragraphs of your argument essay and continue providing reasons and evidence in support of your claim. As you continue drafting the argument, ask yourself:

- In my first two paragraphs, have I established a formal style and an objective tone?
- What specific language can I incorporate to make my writing sound objective?
- Have I established a formal style by avoiding contractions, slang, and popular expressions?

Write your draft on a separate sheet of paper or start a new document.

Conventions

Maintain Subject-Verb Agreement with Correlative Conjunctions

DIRECTIONS Combine the sentences below using the correlative conjunctions given in parentheses. Check for correct subject-verb agreement in your sentences.

1. The eagle was once considered to be a threatened species. The gray wolf was once considered to be a threatened species. (both/and)

____

____

2. Conservationists can repopulate species in the wild. Conservationists can track species in the wild. (either/or)

____

____

3. Geraldo does not have a smartphone. Kelly does not have a smartphone. (neither/nor)

____

____

Students write routinely for a range of tasks, purposes, and audiences. Students practice various conventions of standard English.

Name ______________________________

Benchmark Vocabulary

DIRECTIONS Write a sentence using each word.

commuter gestures

____

____

____

____

Write in Response to Reading

The author of *No Easy Answers: Our Digital World* presents two different points of view about technology on pages 26–37. Review pages 26–31. Using examples the author included, write one paragraph in support of the key idea "Technology is helpful."

____

____

____

____

____

____

____

____

____

____

____

____

____

Students demonstrate contextual understanding of Benchmark Vocabulary. Students read text closely and use text evidence in their written answers.

Name ______________________________

Analyze Elaboration

DIRECTIONS Using evidence from the text, answer the following questions about pages 26–37 from *No Easy Answers: Our Digital World.*

1. How does the author elaborate on his key idea in "Are driverless cars really an improvement over cars with human drivers?"

____

____

____

____

____

2. How does the author elaborate on his key idea in "Is social media destroying our social skills?"

____

____

____

____

____

3. Compare and contrast how the author uses visual features to elaborate on his ideas in the two sections from today's reading.

____

____

____

____

____

Students analyze and respond to literary and informational text.

Name ____________________

Argument Writing: Evaluate the Strength of an Argument Review the draft of your argument essay about the most critical quality of an entrepreneur. As you review and revise your draft, consider:

- Have I provided solid, clearly stated reasons to support my claim?
- Is each piece of evidence closely tied to the claim and reasons?
- Have I organized my ideas clearly and logically for my readers?

Write your draft on a separate sheet of paper or start a new document.

Correct Vague Pronouns with Unclear Antecedents

DIRECTIONS Rewrite the sentences below so that pronouns refer clearly to specific nouns in number and gender.

1. My mother listened to a recording of plays that they acted in long ago.

____

____

2. The playbill gave a description of each cast member and their role in the show.

____

____

3. I also love movies and plays and watch it whenever I have the chance.

____

____

4. They signed their autographs for the fans when the play was over.

____

____

Students write routinely for a range of tasks, purposes, and audiences. Students practice various conventions of standard English.

Name ______________________________

Benchmark Vocabulary

DIRECTIONS Write a sentence using each word.

leisure   aggressive   evaluate

____

____

____

Write in Response to Reading

Reread pages 39–47 of *No Easy Answers*. Has the author written a persuasive text, an informative text, or both? Use details from the text to support your answer.

____

____

____

____

____

____

____

____

____

____

____

Students demonstrate contextual understanding of Benchmark Vocabulary. Students read text closely and use text evidence in their written answers.

Name ____________________

Author's Purpose

DIRECTIONS Using evidence from the text, answer the following questions about *No Easy Answers: Our Digital World.*

1. How does the title "Smart Technology Requires Smart Users" reflect the author's purpose?

2. How does providing general statements about technology on the last two pages affect readers' understanding of the author's points?

Students analyze and respond to literary and informational text.

Name ________________________________

Writing

Argument Writing: Conclude an Argument Review the introduction and body of your argument essay about the most critical quality of an entrepreneur. As you review, identify the key points you made as you developed your reasons. Then write a concluding paragraph in which you sum up these points. Remember, an effective conclusion should go beyond simple summary in order to make an impression on readers and leave them thinking further about the topic.

As you develop your concluding paragraph, consider:

- Which reasons and evidence best support my claim?
- Which of these points is important enough to include in my conclusion?
- What thoughtful question or quotation could I include to end the argument effectively?

Use a separate sheet of paper or start a new document.

Conventions

Correct Vague Pronouns and Ambiguous Antecedents

DIRECTIONS Rewrite the sentences below so that the antecedent of each pronoun is clear.

1. Rick asked Jason if his technology project was finished.

____

____

2. When Maria invited her mother to the science fair, she seemed very excited about it.

____

____

3. When they displayed their projects, they were greeted with applause from them.

____

4. The school principal announced they could show their exhibits again in the spring term.

____

Students write routinely for a range of tasks, purposes, and audiences. Students practice various conventions of standard English.

Name ______________________________

Benchmark Vocabulary

DIRECTIONS Write a sentence using each word.

launch benefits

____

____

____

____

Write in Response to Reading

The authors of *Steve Jobs* and *No Easy Answers* use many sidebars to elaborate on additional topics related to technology. Choose a sidebar from each book and write its description and page number in the space provided. Compare and contrast how the authors have used these sidebars to elaborate or develop their texts.

____

____

____

____

____

____

____

____

____

____

____

____

____

Students demonstrate contextual understanding of Benchmark Vocabulary. Students read text closely and use text evidence in their written answers.

Name ______________________________

Writing

Argument Writing: Conduct Research Use the library and the Internet to find three appropriate sources on the topic of successful entrepreneurs. Read each source carefully to make sure it is both relevant and credible, or trustworthy. Review the criteria for credible sources that your teacher shared with you. Then write an explanation of why each source is credible.

As you conduct research and write explanations, consider:

- Who is the author, and what is the date and place of publication of each source?
- Does each source have enough information related to my writing topic?
- Is the information presented in an objective manner and based on facts?

List your sources below or on a separate sheet of paper or start a new document. Then write your short explanations telling why each source is credible.

Conventions

Use Verb Sequences

DIRECTIONS Rewrite the sentences below, using the correct sequence of verb tenses. Then write two sentences in which you describe actions that took place yesterday and today and actions that will most likely take place tomorrow.

1. Yesterday I take the Number 7 train, today I traveled by another route, and tomorrow I stay at home all day.

____

____

2. The wind is fierce yesterday, but today the weather was calm; tomorrow it is rainy.

____

____

3. ______________________________

____

4. ______________________________

____

Students write routinely for a range of tasks, purposes, and audiences. Students practice various conventions of standard English.

Name ______________________________

Benchmark Vocabulary

DIRECTIONS Write a sentence using each word.

disrupt consecutive

____

____

____

____

Write in Response to Reading

Do you think people should be discouraged from staring at electronic screens right before bed? Using evidence from the article, write a persuasive paragraph for or against the claim that electronic screens before bed are harmful. Write your response below, on a separate sheet of paper, or in a new document.

____

____

____

____

____

____

____

____

____

____

____

____

____

Students demonstrate contextual understanding of Benchmark Vocabulary. Students read text closely and use text evidence in their written answers.

Name ______________________________

Argument Writing: Synthesize Research Revise your draft on the topic of successful entrepreneurs using three additional sources. Evaluate the key ideas in each source and write a brief summary of these ideas. As you revise, aim at incorporating paraphrase and direct quotations into your writing.

As you synthesize information from the three sources, consider:

- What new ideas and evidence are presented in each source?
- How will I summarize the important findings from these sources?
- How does this information affect the claim I made in my draft?
- What materials will I paraphrase, and what statements will I quote?

Write your revised essay on a separate sheet of paper or start a new document.

Use Verb Sequences

DIRECTIONS Rewrite the infinitive form of the verb in parentheses in the perfect tense, progressive tense, or future tense, as appropriate for sentence meaning.

1. It (to rain) for many hours before the skies finally cleared.

____

2. I (to pack) a bag for a beach trip while my sister was checking the forecast.

____

3. The weather reporter (to predict) an entire day of bad weather, but actually it (to clear) by noon.

____

4. The waves (to sparkle) as we rode our bikes down the path. If it is sunny tomorrow, we (to make) an earlier start.

____

Students write routinely for a range of tasks, purposes, and audiences. Students practice various conventions of standard English.

Name ______________________________

Inferred Word Meanings

DIRECTIONS Read the paragraph. Write the meanings of the underlined words and the context clues that help you determine the meanings. Use a dictionary to verify your inferred meanings.

Right after the incident of losing to the team from the next block, Kyle thought of an inventive and original way to win the next tag football game. The kids on his team congregated as a group for practice at the park, and Kyle brought along his hound Bo. Kyle included Bo in the practice by having Bo smell the ball and then bound high and crawl low to find where Kyle tossed or hid the ball. Kyle angled for one last practice by promising a big win at the next game, using Bo as their secret weapon.

1. incident ______________________________
2. inventive ______________________________
3. congregated ______________________________
4. bound ______________________________
5. angled ______________________________

DIRECTIONS Write the parts of speech for the underlined words.

6. Su-Lin thought Kyle's nonsensical idea had many flaws.

   ____

7. Marta sensed that underneath Kyle's tough exterior, he had a heart of gold.

   ____

8. Felipe, an acknowledged math guru, helped Kyle calculate the feasibility of their plan. ____________________

9. Tyler showed Kyle the absolutely safe way for Bo to retrieve the ball from the other team's players. ____________________

10. Which of the above sentences include prepositional phrases? Circle them.

    ____

DIRECTIONS Match selected underlined words from above with definitions.

11. nonsensical	______	**a.** state or degree of being easily done
12. sensed	______	**b.** foolish or untrue
13. feasibility	______	**c.** find and get
14. retrieve	______	**d.** felt

Students apply grade-level word analysis skills.

Name ______________________________

Benchmark Vocabulary

DIRECTIONS Write a sentence using each word.

gadget ambitions

____
____
____
____

Write in Response to Reading

Reread "Screen Time Can Mess with the Body's 'Clock'." Does it present a balanced view of the positive and negative effects of tablet computers? Why or why not? Provide examples from the text to support your argument.

____
____
____
____
____
____
____
____
____
____
____
____
____
____
____

Students demonstrate contextual understanding of Benchmark Vocabulary. Students read text closely and use text evidence in their written answers.

Name ____________________

Evaluate Causes and Effects

DIRECTIONS Using evidence from the text, answer the following questions about *Steve Jobs* and "Screen Time Can Mess with the Body's 'Clock'."

1. Often, the effects a person has on society is known as his or her "legacy." According to the author of *Steve Jobs,* what is Steve Jobs's legacy?

____

____

____

2. How do these two texts, when read together, present a balanced view of the effects of modern technology?

____

____

____

____

____

____

____

____

Students analyze and respond to literary and informational text.

Name ______________________________

Writing

Argument Writing: Citing Sources Think about how you incorporated the ideas of other writers into your draft about the most critical quality of a successful entrepreneur. Review your draft and decide where source citations are needed. Then create a bibliography of works cited.

As you add citations, consider:

- Which ideas and information in my draft are common knowledge?
- Which information did I paraphrase from the work of other writers?
- How can I smoothly work parenthetical citations into my writing?
- Have I recorded all the necessary details for my bibliography?

Write your revised essay on a separate sheet of paper or start a new document. Then create a separate page or document for your bibliography.

Conventions

Use Gerunds and Gerund Phrases

DIRECTIONS Fill in the blank in each sentence below with a gerund or gerund phrase. Then write two new sentences that include gerund phrases.

1. ______________ is an activity that I enjoy on the weekends.

2. My cousins live in the mountains and often go ______________.

3. ____

____

4. ____

____

Students write routinely for a range of tasks, purposes, and audiences. Students practice various conventions of standard English.

Name ______________________________

Benchmark Vocabulary

DIRECTIONS Write a sentence using each word.

browsing trends

Write in Response to Reading

The flow chart on pages 66–67 of *Gadgets and Games* gives a visual representation of the life cycle of a tablet. Using the information on the pages, write a summary, in your own words, of the series of events involved in the life of a tablet. Write your response below, on a separate sheet of paper, or in a new document.

Students demonstrate contextual understanding of Benchmark Vocabulary. Students read text closely and use text evidence in their written answers.

Name ______________________________

Birds and Planes: An Unhappy Rendezvous in the Sky

When you think of geese, gulls, and starlings, one word that probably doesn't come to mind is dangerous. Still, over the years, birds like these have caused people plenty of serious injuries and even deaths. In 1996, for example, a flock of birds killed 34 people in the Netherlands. In 1960, starlings were responsible for the deaths of 62 people in Massachusetts. Geese killed 24 people in Alaska, and pigeons killed 31 people in Ethiopia.

These people weren't quacked to death or pecked to pieces. They were on airplanes that collided with flocks of birds. Obviously, a collision like that is a serious problem for the birds. It's hard to survive an impact with tons of metal traveling hundreds of miles an hour. Yet when birds are sucked into a plane's engines, it's also an issue for the plane and people on board. In the worst cases, the birds' bodies cause engine failure and a plane to crash. Even when the collision doesn't result in a plane crash, it can cause major damages and expenses. Plane-bird collisions cost more than $1 billion a year in repairs and flight delays.

The risk of bird-plane collisions is increasing. Laws that protect birds and their habitats have gotten stronger recently, so there are more birds around airports than ever. More birds often mean more accidents. Air traffic is also increasing, and in recent years, airplane engines have gotten quieter. Quieter engines give birds less time to move away from approaching planes. One study shows that bird-plane collisions are four times more common today than they were in 1990.

By now you might be thinking twice about boarding an airplane again, but you can relax. For one thing, experts are working to reduce the number of crashes. Personnel at some airports report the use of sirens, gas-filled tubes, or predators to scare flocks away from runways. Screenlike guards on engines can also keep larger birds from being pulled inside.

Even though collisions are more likely than they used to be, the odds are in your favor. Only a tiny percentage of flights hits any birds at all. And, as the author of "*It's a Bird, It's a Plane . . .*" explains, "Most 'bird strikes' don't damage an aircraft at all." What's the bottom line in all of this? There's no need to worry about plane-bird collisions—as long as you're an airline passenger and not a bird!

Students read text closely to determine what the text says.

Sleuth Work

Name ______________________________

Gather Evidence On page 346, underline text details that elaborate on the problem introduced by the author.

Gather Evidence: Extend Your Ideas Read through the underlined details. How do they help you understand the author's main point?

____

____

____

Ask Questions Write two questions you have for travelers about how this problem affects their air travel.

____

____

Ask Questions: Extend Your Ideas Choose one of the two questions you have for airport personnel. Find details in the text that give you an idea of what the answers might be. Write them below.

____

____

____

Make Your Case On page 346, circle text that reveals the solutions mentioned by the author.

Make Your Case: Extend Your Ideas What final message does the author give to the reader about the dangers involved with collisions between airplanes and birds?

____

____

____

Students read text closely to determine what the text says.

Name ______________________________

Writing

Argument Writing: Conduct Research to Gather and Synthesize Evidence
Imagine you are in charge of technology for a school district. The current year's budget allows for one major technology purchase. Make a recommendation for a technology your school district should pursue. Support your claim with clear reasons and relevant evidence from *Steve Jobs, No Easy Answers: Our Digital World,* and other credible sources. As you conduct research, consider these issues:

- What is the purpose and focus of my research?
- Which types of additional sources will likely yield relevant information?
- Which information should I record on note cards to help me later when I start writing?
- What is the necessary information for a bibliographic entry?

Keep a record of the sources you used on a separate sheet of paper or start a new document.

Conventions

Use Participles and Participial Phrases

DIRECTIONS: Complete the first two sentences below with a phrase in which the participle ends in *-ing*. Then complete the last sentence with a participle ending in *-ed* or *-en*.

1. ______________ is my favorite thing to do after school.
2. I've thought of ______________ in a school research report.
3. The article I read was ______________ from a famous book about planets and other heavenly bodies.

Students write routinely for a range of tasks, purposes, and audiences. Students practice various conventions of standard English.

Name ____________________

Benchmark Vocabulary

DIRECTIONS Write a sentence using each word.

interface microscopic capacity strategy

Write in Response to Reading

Reread *Gadgets and Games*, pages 78–79. Describe how the software development process works in order to design a complete operating system.

Students demonstrate contextual understanding of Benchmark Vocabulary. Students read text closely and use text evidence in their written answers.

Name ______________________________

Writing

Argument Writing: Plan and Organize an Argument Using information from the various sources you have gathered, draft a claim about the type of technology your school system should purchase. Then create an outline for a draft including an introduction, body paragraphs, and a conclusion.

As you plan your argument essay, consider:

- What claim can I make based upon the research I did?
- Which reasons strongly support this claim and will appear in the parts of the outline headed by Roman numerals?
- Which supporting points and details will I indicate with capital letters and Arabic numerals?

Use a separate sheet of paper or start a new document.

Conventions

Use Infinitives and Infinitive Phrases

DIRECTIONS Rewrite the sentences below, replacing the underlined word with the appropriate infinitive. Then write one new sentence that includes an infinitive phrase, and a related sentence with only an infinitive.

1. Playing soccer professionally would be a fantastic career.

____

2. I love shooting baskets with my friends after school.

____

3. ______________________________

____

Students write routinely for a range of tasks, purposes, and audiences. Students practice various conventions of standard English.

Name ______________________________

Benchmark Vocabulary

DIRECTIONS Write a sentence using each word.

suitable fabricated

____

____

____

____

Write in Response to Reading

Prepare an outline for "Prototypes and Testing" on pages 82–87. Be sure to include the section head, subheadings, and a central idea for each subheading. Write your answer below, on a separate sheet of paper, or in a new document.

____

____

____

____

____

____

____

____

____

____

____

____

____

Students demonstrate contextual understanding of Benchmark Vocabulary. Students read text closely and use text evidence in their written answers.

Name ______________________________

Connect Central Idea and Elaboration

DIRECTIONS Using evidence from the text, answer the following questions about pages 82–95 of *Gadgets and Games.*

1. Read about prototype testing and evaluation on pages 82–83. How does the author help readers understand how important these steps are in the development of gadgets?

____

____

____

____

____

____

2. How does the author elaborate on the topic of debugging software on page 85?

____

____

____

____

____

Students analyze and respond to literary and informational text.

Name ____________________

Writing

Argument Writing: Draft an Argument Review the claim and outline you have written about the type of technology that should be purchased by the school district. Then begin drafting an introduction, body, and conclusion to your argument essay.

As you draft your argument essay, consider:

- How will I make my reasoning compelling and persuasive to the reader?
- Which pieces of evidence from my sources will make my argument strong?
- Which sentences from my sources are most quotable?
- Which ideas will I need to paraphrase?

Use a separate sheet of paper or start a new document.

Conventions

Use Interjections in Sentences

DIRECTIONS Add an appropriate stand-alone interjection before each sentence below. Then write two new sentences that include an interjection.

1. ____________________ The line for this movie showing is incredibly long.

2. ____________________ I have to get this painful splinter out of my finger.

3. ____________________

____

4. ____________________

____

Students write routinely for a range of tasks, purposes, and audiences. Students practice various conventions of standard English.

Name ______________________________

Benchmark Vocabular

DIRECTIONS Write a sentence using each word.

guarantee   malfunctioning   obsolete

____

____

____

____

____

____

Write in Response to Reading

Reread *Gadgets and Games*, pages 104–107. Write a paragraph explaining, in simple language, the two most environmentally responsible options users have at the end of a gadget's life cycle. Use details from the text to explain how these two options work. Write your answer below, on a separate sheet of paper, or in a new document.

____

____

____

____

____

____

____

____

____

____

Students demonstrate contextual understanding of Benchmark Vocabulary. Students read text closely and use text evidence in their written answers.

Name ____________________

Writing

Argument Writing: Revise an Argument Review your draft of an argument in favor of the type of technology the school system should purchase. Then revise your argument so that your claim and reasons are supported with credible evidence. As you revise your essay, consider:

- Is my reasoning logical and well-supported with evidence?
- Have I provided clear transitions between ideas and between paragraphs?
- Have I maintained a formal style and objective tone throughout the writing?
- Does my conclusion follow logically from my claim and reasons?

Use a separate sheet of paper or start a new document.

Conventions

Spell Correctly: Adding Suffixes to Words That End in *y*

DIRECTIONS Rewrite the sentences below, replacing the underlined infinitive of the verb with a gerund or participle. Then write two sentences of your own using a gerund or participle.

1. To beautify the front yard will require planting some colorful flowers.

____

____

2. Cold weather in springtime is known to delay the blooming of some flowers.

____

____

3. ____________________

____

4. ____________________

____

Students write routinely for a range of tasks, purposes, and audiences. Students practice various conventions of standard English.

Name ______________________________

Shades of Meaning

DIRECTIONS Read the word pairs. Write the word that suggests an image and conveys a tone or attitude. You may use a dictionary to verify word meanings.

1. discover, unearth ____________________
2. slither, wriggle ____________________
3. thwart, oppose ____________________
4. sighting, glimpse ____________________
5. dance, boogie ____________________
6. mutter, whisper ____________________

DIRECTIONS Read the paragraph. Write a substitute word for the underlined verbs that will fit the context and convey tone. Choose from this list of words: *examined, hustled, surveyed, organized, verified, observed.*

Coach Ellen always followed a pregame ritual. First, she wanted to ensure that everyone would have a chance to play, so she checked the roster methodically. Nan would be the lead-off batter followed by Arjun and Lisa. If there were no outs at that point, the twins would follow them. She then put the equipment in the correct places and made sure that Jim's special bat was included. Coach Ellen looked at the field to make sure there was no debris. Finally, she quickly walked to the dugout to set out healthy snacks and beverages for right after the game.

1. followed ____________________
2. checked ____________________
3. put ____________________
4. made sure ____________________
5. looked at ____________________
6. walked ____________________

Students apply grade-level word analysis skills.

Benchmark Vocabulary

Name ______________________________

DIRECTIONS Write a sentence using each word.

capacity guarantee perfection

____

____

____

____

____

____

Write in Response to Reading

Reread pages 42–43 of *Steve Jobs*. How did Jobs's own advice come in handy for him in his business career? Provide examples from the text to support your answer. Write your answer below, on a separate sheet of paper, or in a new document.

____

____

____

____

____

____

____

____

____

____

Students demonstrate contextual understanding of Benchmark Vocabulary. Students read text closely and use text evidence in their written answers.

Name ______________________________

Elaboration and Author's Purpose

DIRECTIONS Using evidence from the text, answer the following questions about *Gadgets and Games* and *Steve Jobs.*

1. Give an example of how the author of *Gadgets and Games* uses photographs and other visuals to elaborate on his purpose for writing.

____
____
____
____

2. What purpose is supported by the example you gave in Question 1?

____
____
____
____

3. Give an example of how the author of *Steve Jobs* uses photographs and other visuals to elaborate on his purpose for writing.

____
____
____
____

4. What purpose is supported by the example you gave in Question 3?

____
____
____
____

Students analyze and respond to literary or informational text.

Name ____________________

Writing

Argument Writing: Edit and Proofread an Argument Edit and proofread your draft of the argument in favor of the type of technology you think the school district should purchase. As you edit and proofread your essay, consider these points:

- Are all clauses complete and clear, with correct punctuation?
- Have I maintained a formal style throughout the writing?
- Have I included information about the author, title, and publication of each source, including bibliographic information used for Web sites?
- Is it clear where I have paraphrased and where I have directly quoted another writer's words?

Use a separate sheet of paper or start a new document to edit your argument.

Conventions

Use Standard English: Pronoun Case

DIRECTIONS Complete each of the sentences below by choosing either *who* or *whom*.

1. Who/Whom is the guest speaker at today's assembly?

2. To who/whom should I address this speech of welcome?

3. The guest for who/whom we are waiting is an expert in technology.

4. Who/Whom has a question for the distinguished visitor?

Students write routinely for a range of tasks, purposes, and audiences. Students practice various conventions of standard English.

Name ________________________________

Benchmark Vocabulary

DIRECTIONS Write a sentence using each word.

confident suitable

Write in Response to Reading

Reread pages 26 and 27 of *No Easy Answers: Our Digital World*. Write an argument essay about driverless cars and whether or not you think they are a good idea. Use text evidence to support your answer. Write your answer below, on a separate sheet of paper, or in a new document.

Students demonstrate contextual understanding of Benchmark Vocabulary. Students read text closely and use text evidence in their written answers.

Name ________________________________

Writing

Argument Writing: Exploring Opposing Arguments Before you participate in the video debate about purchasing a particular type of technology, you will be doing some additional planning. Brainstorm a sensible counterargument that could be made in response to your argument. Make some notes about a good response to this counterargument, based on reasons and evidence you have already discussed in your essay. Use a separate sheet of paper or start a new document.

Conventions

Use Strategies to Improve Expression

DIRECTIONS Each sentence below contains an error in grammar or usage. Correct the error by rewriting the sentence on the lines below.

1. Although students or teachers can help us improve a presentation.

2. Since I am speaking in public for the first time tomorrow, I practice first.

3. I been informed of the schedule and are ready to perform.

4. My notes on the topic is detailed and will help me remember the important points.

Students write routinely for a range of tasks, purposes, and audiences. Students practice various conventions of standard English.

Name ______________________________

Benchmark Vocabulary

DIRECTIONS Write a sentence using each word.

retracted detach external maximum

Write in Response to Reading

Describe how the author structures the story's plot in Chapter 1, pages 13–31. Identify a goal or conflict for the main character and the outcome or resolution. Provide examples from the text to support your answer. Write your answer below, on a separate sheet of paper, or in a new document.

Students demonstrate contextual understanding of Benchmark Vocabulary. Students read text closely and use text evidence in their written answers.

Name ______________________________

Writing

Informative/Explanatory Writing: Examine Features and Purpose of an Informational Brochure Examine the informational brochure that your teacher provides. Then write a paragraph describing the topic of the brochure, how it is formatted, and the kinds of graphics that are used. Explain in your paragraph how the brochure engages readers and describe the kind of language the writer uses. Write your paragraph on a separate sheet of paper or start a new document.

Conventions

Use Commas with Interjections and Tag Questions

DIRECTIONS Rewrite each sentence, adding commas where needed to show interjections and tag questions.

1. Ben is going to the park later right?

____

2. Hey I have never seen such a scary movie!

____

3. Oops the new glass slipped out of my hand.

____

4. A dog can see better in the dark than a human can't it?

____

5. I finished my homework with plenty of time to spare didn't I?

____

Students write routinely for a range of tasks, purposes, and audiences. Students practice various conventions of standard English.

Name ____________________

Context Clues

DIRECTIONS Read the paragraph. Write the meanings of the underlined words and the specific context clues that helped you determine the meaning. Context clues can include definition, explanation, synonym, signal words, antonym, or overall meaning. Use a dictionary to help you.

Selling tickets to your school's fundraiser sounds boring, and it isn't the most stimulating thing to do on warm spring days after school. Throw in an incentive, such as a season pass to the football games, and you've got yourself a deal. My class was split into five teams, and someone even drew one of those large life-sized thermometers with a notch that inched up daily to our goal. For a while the five teams were neck and neck in points earned. Then two of us led the pack while the three laggards stayed behind in the cellar. Forget about sports, forget about dinner, and forget about homework. Yes, you heard me. Our team just wanted to forge ahead and win the coveted prize that the other teams wanted so badly. It spurred and galvanized us like nothing in the world.

1. stimulating ____________________
2. incentive ____________________
3. laggards ____________________
4. coveted ____________________
5. galvanized ____________________

DIRECTIONS Write the meanings of the underlined words in each sentence. Use context clues and a dictionary, glossary, or thesaurus for assistance.

6. Ben and Maria were the inspiring co-captains who cheered us on and made us feel like essential team members by telling us that our efforts would help our team win. ____________________
7. Their competitive spirit and absolute authority over us subordinates were forces that pushed us to sell until we were hawking tickets all over town.

   ____
8. Within our six-person squad, Katie and Luis took a commanding lead as the top sellers. ____________________
9. Al and I, with our low ticket sales, vied for the title of least enterprising member, and we had no excuse for being so lazy and unproductive. ____________________
10. Team Five and Team Six both amassed nearly 1,000 points, and we intensely and ardently hoped a tiebreaker would be unnecessary.

   ____

Students apply grade-level word analysis skills.

Name ______________________________

DIRECTIONS Write a sentence using each word.

confronted diminished anticipating

____

____

____

____

____

____

Write in Response to Reading

How is the character of Emmett introduced to the reader on page 65 of the story? How is this new character likely to have an effect on the plot? Provide text evidence to support your opinion. Write your answer below, on a separate sheet of paper, or in a new document.

____

____

____

____

____

____

____

____

____

____

____

Students demonstrate contextual understanding of Benchmark Vocabulary. Students read text closely and use text evidence in their written answers.

Name ______________________________

Text Structure and Plot

DIRECTIONS Using evidence from the text, answer the following questions about *George's Cosmic Treasure Hunt.*

1. Reread the text on pages 40–41. How does the author use the compare and contrast text structure?

____

____

____

2. On pages 44–46, what is the author's purpose for having Annie say good-bye to Freddy the pig?

____

____

____

3. On page 60, what text structure does the author use in "The Voyage Through the History of Human Thought"?

____

____

____

____

4. Give an example of how the author uses a cause-and-effect relationship to develop the plot of the story.

____

____

____

____

Students analyze and respond to literary and informational text.

Name ______________________________

Writing

Informative/Explanatory Writing: Research a Topic Begin your research on the Big Bang theory by identifying reliable print and online sources. Write the names of these sources of information and explain how you know that each is a reliable source with accurate information. List your sources on the lines below. Use a separate sheet of paper or start a new document if you need more space.

____

____

____

____

____

Conventions

Use Relative Pronouns

DIRECTIONS Choose the relative pronoun that best completes each sentence. Each pronoun is used only once.

that	which	who	whom	whose

1. Jennifer bought a new dress, ________ is bright pink.

2. The woman ________ drove me to school is my Aunt Dana.

3. Mrs. Ratliff, ________ I like very much, is the new school principal.

4. My brother, ________ leg is broken, is a football player.

5. The chain ________ fell off my bike was difficult to replace.

Students write routinely for a range of tasks, purposes, and audiences. Students practice various conventions of standard English.

Name ______________________________

Benchmark Vocabulary

DIRECTIONS Write a sentence using each word.

confirmed extraordinary terrestrial resume

Write in Response to Reading

How would you describe the relationship between Annie and Emmett? Cite text evidence to support your answer.

Write your answer below, on a separate sheet of paper, or in a new document.

Students demonstrate contextual understanding of Benchmark Vocabulary. Students read text closely and use text evidence in their written answers.

Name ______________________________

Nature Copycats!

Twenty-first century inventions allow us to do things that once were thought to be science fiction. We launch people into space, replace worn-out or diseased body parts, and have immediate access to vast amounts of information on our phones. Humans are the greatest inventors on Earth, right? Well . . . maybe not.

An invention is a solution to a problem. Since the first bacteria appeared on this planet 3.8 billion years ago, the ability to solve problems has meant the difference between life and death for living organisms. Through adaptation, animals, plants, and microbes have found different ways to adapt to diverse environments on Earth.

Today, scientists in the field of biomimicry focus on the natural world as the source of inspiration to solve human problems. *Biomimicry* comes from *bio-*, meaning "life," and *mimic*, meaning "to imitate." Consider, for example, how the Wright brothers' observations of flying birds inspired their design of early airplanes.

Here are several more recent examples to explore:

- Certain bacteria living in oil pipelines get energy and food by breaking down oil. Engineers now use these bacteria to clean pipelines and oil storage tanks and clean up oil spills.
- The structure of butterfly wings repels dirt and causes water to roll off them. Engineers copy that structure when formulating dirt-resistant paints and textiles, including a well-known brand of jeans.
- Many species of winged insects use their panel-like wings to capture solar radiation and to move air in ways that produce remarkable flying ability. An innovative sailboat design mimics this technique to take advantage of wind and solar energy, the two most abundant and inexhaustible energy sources on Earth.
- Because their fibers are arranged in the direction of forces acting on them, tree trunks are resistant to breaking. For whom has this discovery been useful? It has been especially useful to engineers who replicate this structure to build composite materials. Cars designed with these principles are as crash-safe as conventional cars, but up to 30 percent lighter.
- Biomimicry has produced many inventions that produce sustainable energy, such as the bioWAVE—units mounted to the ocean floor that convert wave motion to electricity. The way in which the units are attached to the sea floor and their ability to move and rotate to capture wave motion are modeled after seaweed.

Plants and animals have inspired thousands of other technologies. So, the next time you have a problem, you might ask: How does nature solve it?

Students read text closely to determine what the text says.

Name ____________________

Gather Evidence Which words or phrases does the author use to describe what scientists do to solve problems? Circle the words in the passage.

Gather Evidence: Extend Your Ideas How do these words help you understand the scientific process behind biomimicry?

____

____

____

Ask Questions Write three questions that can be answered by reading the text.

____

____

____

Ask Questions: Extend Your Ideas Imagine that you are the inventor of one of the example inventions mentioned in the text. How would you answer these questions?

____

____

____

____

____

Make Your Case What is the purpose of biomimicry?

____

____

Make Your Case: Extend Your Ideas How would you describe the benefits of using biomimicry?

____

____

____

Students read text closely to determine what the text says.

Name ____

Informative/Explanatory Writing: Researching and Note Taking Using the source list you created in Lesson 2, identify information from your sources that is relevant to the Big Bang theory. You will expand upon your original list of sources and choose those that you will use for your research. The sources you use should provide the information you need to write a brochure. Write your sources on the lines below.

____

____

____

____

____

Use Restrictive Relative Clauses

DIRECTIONS Circle the restrictive relative clause in each sentence below.

1. I ate the lunch that my dad made for me.
2. The man who works at the auto shop gave my car a tune-up.
3. The hurricane that was very strong did a lot of damage.
4. The woman who works at the art museum gave us a tour.
5. I visited my friend whose dog just had puppies.

Students write routinely for a range of tasks, purposes, and audiences. Students practice various conventions of standard English.

Name ______________________

Benchmark Vocabulary

DIRECTIONS Write a sentence using each word.

fruitless affirmative scaffolding

Write in Response to Reading

What information do you learn about Eric in Chapters 6–7, pages 104–147? How does this help you understand the plot?

Students demonstrate contextual understanding of Benchmark Vocabulary. Students read text closely and use text evidence in their written answers.

Name ______________________

Writing

Informative/Explanatory Writing: Note Taking Using the sources you identified in previous lessons, take notes about the Big Bang theory. You will use these notes to write your brochure about the Big Bang theory. Paraphrase all information in your notes, except for any text that you plan to quote directly in your writing. Write your notes on a separate sheet of paper or start a new document.

Conventions

Use Nonrestrictive Relative Clauses

DIRECTIONS Circle the nonrestrictive relative clause in each sentence below.

1. Wendy and Maya played a new board game, which they bought last week.

2. My friend Jorge, who moved to Texas last year, likes to play baseball.

3. Amir donated old clothes to charity, which helped a lot of people.

4. My sister, who is a junior in high school, just got her driver's license.

5. Kelly, who doesn't like pizza, had dinner with my family last night.

Students write routinely for a range of tasks, purposes, and audiences. Students practice various conventions of standard English.

Name ________________________

Benchmark Vocabulary

DIRECTIONS Write a sentence using each word.

threshold originated

____

____

____

____

Write in Response to Reading

How does the author use dialogue to engage the reader in the text? Give text examples. Write your answer below, on a separate sheet of paper, or in a new document.

____

____

____

____

____

____

____

____

____

____

____

____

____

____

Students demonstrate contextual understanding of Benchmark Vocabulary. Students read text closely and use text evidence in their written answers.

Name ______________________________

Language and Word Choice

DIRECTIONS Using evidence from the text, answer the following questions about *George's Cosmic Treasure Hunt*.

1. Give an example of how the author uses different kinds of sentences in the informational text. Explain how using a pattern of questions and statements helps the reader understand the information.

____

____

____

____

____

2. What is the author's purpose in using teenage language for Cosmos? Provide a text example.

____

____

____

____

____

3. The author uses a conversational, casual style of language in the dialogue between the characters. Describe why you think the author chose this style.

____

____

____

____

____

Students analyze and respond to literary and informational text.

Name ____________________

Writing

Informative/Explanatory Writing: Organize Ideas Take your notes about the Big Bang theory from Lesson 4 and organize them into an outline. Classify the information into groups, with headings that can become subheadings in your brochure about the Big Bang theory. Write your outline on a separate sheet of paper or start a new document.

Conventions

Use Restrictive Elements

DIRECTIONS Circle the restrictive element in each sentence below.

1. The bowl with the red and pink flowers contains the gluten-free snacks.

2. The four moms in the yellow T-shirts organized the entire party.

3. The boy who dressed up as Jupiter won a prize for the best space-themed costume.

4. The person who is wearing the crazy glasses is the DJ for the party.

5. The girl who is dressed up as a computer takes a lot of programming classes.

Students write routinely for a range of tasks, purposes, and audiences. Students practice various conventions of standard English.

Name ____

Benchmark Vocabulary

DIRECTIONS Write a sentence using each word.

frigid profound

Write in Response to Reading

How does the author use sequence or chronological order to structure the plot in Chapters 10 and 11? How does the event sequence help move the plot forward? Write your response below, on a separate sheet of paper, or in a new document.

Students demonstrate contextual understanding of Benchmark Vocabulary. Students read text closely and use text evidence in their written answers.

Name ______________________________

Writing

Informative/Explanatory Writing: Develop a Topic Write two informative paragraphs about a place on Earth or in space that you would like to visit one day. Develop your topic by adding facts, examples, definitions, and other information to describe and explain this place. Write your paragraphs on a separate sheet of paper or start a new document.

Conventions

Use Nonrestrictive or Parenthetical Elements

DIRECTIONS Rewrite each sentence, adding punctuation to set off the nonrestrictive element.

1. Mom took us to a restaurant Susan's favorite for dinner.

____

2. They changed their menu again.

____

3. I had a chicken sandwich not something I have ordered before.

____

4. Mac had the new very large plate of spaghetti.

____

5. After ordering dessert I realized I ate too much!

____

Students write routinely for a range of tasks, purposes, and audiences. Students practice various conventions of standard English.

Name ______________________________

Connotation and Denotation

DIRECTIONS Replace the underlined word in each sentence with a word from the Word Bank that has a similar denotation but a negative connotation. Not all the words will be used.

Word Bank

leaked	gripe	fishy	mock	doormat	rowdy
scrawny	manipulate	bitter	chicken	bland	smirk

1. The city official reported information about the building plan at a town hall meeting. **1.** ______________

2. If I act like a servant to my older sister, she'll always treat me like one. **2.** ______________

3. This spaghetti sauce tastes unseasoned and could use some chili flakes. **3.** ______________

4. There is something suspicious about this room full of balloons. **4.** ______________

5. My smart collie can influence me into giving her treats with just a look. **5.** ______________

6. It's not polite to tease toddlers who haven't yet learned correct grammar. **6.** ______________

7. Would you be upset if waves ruined the sandcastle that took you four hours to build? **7.** ______________

8. Does it do any good to complain about the same thing over and over? **8.** ______________

9. That slim squirrel must have forgotten where it buried all of its nuts. **9.** ______________

10. Our neighborhood block party can become loud. **10.** ______________

Students apply grade-level word analysis skills.

Name ____________________

Benchmark Vocabulary

DIRECTIONS Write a sentence using each word.

disbelief telltale functioning

Write in Response to Reading

What role does the author have Mabel play in the story? Write your response below, on a separate sheet of paper, or in a new document.

Students demonstrate contextual understanding of Benchmark Vocabulary. Students read text closely and use text evidence in their written answers.

Name ______________________________

Text Structure

DIRECTIONS Using evidence from the text, answer the following questions about *George's Cosmic Treasure Hunt.*

1. What conflict, or problem, does Mabel recognize in Chapter 12? How does she resolve this conflict?

2. Why does the author include the informational text section on page 243?

3. In the narrative in Chapter 14, Eric explains what the term *Goldilocks Zone* means. Why does the author provide an informational text section about the same topic on pages 246–247?

Students analyze and respond to literary and informational text.

Name ______________________________

Writing

Informative/Explanatory Writing: Write an Introduction Write an introduction for the two paragraphs you wrote in Lesson 6 about a place you would like to visit on Earth or in space. Make sure you clearly state the topic or thesis statement, provide relevant facts about the topic, and capture the reader's attention. Write your introduction on a separate sheet of paper or start a new document.

Conventions

Use Commas with Nonrestrictive or Parenthetical Elements

DIRECTIONS Rewrite each sentence below, adding commas to set off the nonrestrictive element.

1. Matthew was looking forward to going on vacation to Key West with his family.

____

2. He needed to finish packing including his sandals and swim trunks before he could leave.

____

3. He packed his swim goggles which were blue in case he needed them.

____

4. Tasha Matthew's sister packed five pairs of sandals.

____

5. It was Saturday the day before Matthew's birthday when they finally left for the airport.

____

Students write routinely for a range of tasks, purposes, and audiences. Students practice various conventions of standard English.

Name ____________________

Benchmark Vocabulary

DIRECTIONS Write a sentence using each word.

humanity   cornerstone

____

____

____

____

Write in Response to Reading

How does the author develop the theme of relationships in the story? Provide text evidence to support your answer. Write your answer below, on a separate sheet of paper, or in a new document.

____

____

____

____

____

____

Students demonstrate contextual understanding of Benchmark Vocabulary. Students read text closely and use text evidence in their written answers.

Name ________________________________

Writing

Informative/Explanatory Writing: Select Images/Graphics/Multimedia Choose or create your own media to support the paragraphs you wrote for Lessons 6 and 7. Remember to use only reliable, appropriate sources and correctly cite all of your sources. Write your list of media on a separate sheet of paper or start a new document.

Conventions

Use Parentheses to Set Off Nonrestrictive or Parenthetical Elements

DIRECTIONS Rewrite each sentence below, adding parentheses to set off the nonrestrictive element.

1. The Colorado River which runs through the Grand Canyon provides water to seven states.

   ____

2. Many cities such as Phoenix and Las Vegas rely on the Colorado River for their survival.

   ____

3. The Colorado River begins in the very beautiful Rocky Mountains.

   ____

4. Kaila my friend since fourth grade has been rafting on the Colorado River.

   ____

5. Rafting especially on the Colorado River sounds like fun.

   ____

Students write routinely for a range of tasks, purposes, and audiences. Students practice various conventions of standard English.

Name ______________________

Benchmark Vocabulary

DIRECTIONS Write a sentence using each word.

maximum threshold

Write in Response to Reading

Why do you think the author chose to use a combination of literary text and informational text structures in this book? Was it effective? Why or why not?

Students demonstrate contextual understanding of Benchmark Vocabulary. Students read text closely and use text evidence in their written answers.

Name ________________________

Text Structure

DIRECTIONS Using evidence from the text, answer the following questions about *George's Cosmic Treasure Hunt.*

1. Provide text evidence to show how the author uses dialogue to develop the characters and plot of the story.

2. Find a place in the text where the author makes scientific or informational content easier for the reader to understand. How does the author organize the text in your example?

3. Why do you think the author chose to call the reference book *The User's Guide to the Universe?*

Students analyze and respond to literary and informational text.

Name ____________________________________

Writing

Informative/Explanatory Writing: Write a Conclusion Write a conclusion for the paragraphs you wrote in Lessons 6 and 7. Make sure your conclusion includes:

- a restatement of the main idea
- a summary of the most important details from the paragraphs
- a final statement that leaves a lasting impression on the reader

Use a separate sheet of paper or start a new document.

Conventions

Use Dashes with Nonrestrictive or Parenthetical Elements

DIRECTIONS Rewrite each sentence below, adding dashes to set off the nonrestrictive element.

1. My aunt who loves to bake is coming to visit over the holidays.

____

2. My friend Jake who is in fifth grade wins every swimming meet he enters.

____

3. The aurora borealis the northern lights is a beautiful sight to see in the night sky.

____

4. Harriet Tubman a conductor on the Underground Railroad served as a scout in the Civil War.

____

5. The first cellular phone call made from a street corner in Manhattan took place in 1973.

____

Students write routinely for a range of tasks, purposes, and audiences. Students practice various conventions of standard English.

Name ____________________

Benchmark Vocabulary

DIRECTIONS Write a sentence using the word.

predecessors

____

____

Write in Response to Reading

Reread pages 120–122 of *A Bright Idea*. How did life change after the first light sources were invented? Use details from the text to support your answer. Write your answer below, on a separate sheet of paper, or in a new document.

____

____

____

____

____

____

____

____

____

____

____

____

Students demonstrate contextual understanding of Benchmark Vocabulary. Students read text closely and use text evidence in their written answers.

Name ____________________

Writing

Informative/Explanatory Writing: Word Choice Choose an invention that you use in your everyday life that you want to write about. Write two informative paragraphs about that invention. Remember to use precise, formal language and define domain-specific terms that may be unfamiliar to your audience. Use a separate sheet of paper or start a new document.

Conventions

Combine Sentences Using Restrictive and Nonrestrictive Elements

DIRECTIONS Combine the two sentences for each item by using restrictive and nonrestrictive elements.

1. Andy drove to the store. He sang his favorite song.

____

____

2. I dropped my cell phone last week. The screen cracked.

____

____

3. Jane went to the mall. She bought a new pair of jeans.

____

____

4. Joey and his family took a trip to the Grand Canyon. The Grand Canyon is my favorite vacation spot.

____

____

5. My sister Anna is a high school tennis star. She spends all of her free time practicing.

____

____

Students write routinely for a range of tasks, purposes, and audiences. Students practice various conventions of standard English.

Name ____________________

Benchmark Vocabulary

DIRECTIONS Write a sentence using each word.

safeguard firsthand illuminated

Write in Response to Reading

Reread page 135 of *A Bright Idea*. How did Joseph Swan, another inventor working on creating a light bulb, receive recognition for his work, and what did this mean for Edison? Use details from the text to support your answer. Write your answer below, on a separate sheet of paper, or in a new document.

Students demonstrate contextual understanding of Benchmark Vocabulary. Students read text closely and use text evidence in their written answers.

Name ______________________________

Informative/Explanatory Writing: Use Transitions Think about how the writer uses transition words and phrases to show relationships in *A Bright Idea*. Add transitions to the paragraphs you wrote about an invention you use every day in Lesson 10. You can use transitions to show the following relationships:

- Cause and effect
- Time
- Place
- Compare and contrast

Use a separate sheet of paper or start a new document.

Ensure Subject-Verb Agreement with Intervening Elements

DIRECTIONS Circle the verb that shows agreement with the subject in each sentence.

1. Jamie—who has four nieces—(love / loves) to babysit.
2. Stan—who is one of my favorite uncles—(is / are) coming over for dinner tonight.
3. Every Monday morning, my friends who stay up too late (has / have) trouble waking up for school.
4. Sam and Marco, who both play soccer, (is / are) going away to camp next week.
5. Danita, who is one of my best friends, (need / needs) help with her Spanish homework tonight.

Students write routinely for a range of tasks, purposes, and audiences. Students practice various conventions of standard English.

Name ______________________

Word Analysis

Multiple-Meaning Words

DIRECTIONS Write an example of a homonym and a homograph in the chart. Tell whether the spellings, pronunciations, and meanings of the two homonyms are the same or different. Repeat for the two homographs.

Multiple-Meaning Word	Spelling	Pronunciation	Meaning
Homonym Example: **1.** ______	**2.**	**3.**	**4.**
Homograph Example: **5.** ______	**6.**	**7.**	**8.**

DIRECTIONS Circle two words in each sentence that are multiple-meaning words. Then write the part of speech for each.

9. If this bathroom scale doesn't lie, I'll be able to scale that wall easily.

______

10. Before you play that piano measure again, tell me how to measure this shirt.

______

11. Give me a minute, and then I'll help you replace that minute part in the computer game. ______

12. Would you please run to the store and buy some jam that I can store for a long time? ______

13. A new mobile application will help me post my job application. ______

DIRECTIONS Write a word from the following list to complete each sentence: *accessory, program, offensive, measures, objects.* Some words will be used more than once.

14. Colin ______ to approving the new schedule because it cuts into recess time.

15. Kate and Tanya, who were third on the recital ______, played a piano duet.

16. The ______ team watched a replay of last week's game before practicing with the defensive squad.

17. I will ______ the nightlights to turn on at 8 p.m. each evening.

18. Dad used equal ______ of milk and ice cream to make a shake.

19. She cleared up the ______ smell in the cellar with a room spray.

20. Brian accused Lucy of being a/an ______ in the planning of his surprise birthday party.

Students apply grade-level word analysis skills.

Name ______________________

Benchmark Vocabulary

DIRECTIONS Write a sentence using each word.

fixtures appliances evolve

Write in Response to Reading

Reread page 142 of *A Bright Idea.* How have light fixtures and bulbs changed since the days of Thomas Edison? Use details from the text to support your answer. Write your answer below, on a separate sheet of paper, or in a new document.

Students demonstrate contextual understanding of Benchmark Vocabulary. Students read text closely and use text evidence in their written answers.

Name ______________________________

Text Structure

DIRECTIONS Using evidence from the text, answer the following questions about pages 140–141 of *A Bright Idea.*

1. How does the author structure the text in "Electricity Changes the World" on page 140? Explain.

2. What text structure appears in "Electricity in the Home" on page 141? Explain.

3. What words or phrases does the author use to help the reader know the text structure being used on page 141?

Students analyze and respond to literary and informational text.

Name ______________________________

Writing

Informative/Explanatory Writing: Write a Cause-and-Effect Paragraph Use a cause-and-effect structure to write a paragraph about how life would be different without electricity. Write your paragraph below, on a separate sheet of paper, or in a new document.

____

____

____

____

Conventions

Use Verb Tenses

DIRECTIONS Circle the verb that shows the correct tense to use in each sentence.

1. Emily (was going / will be going) to Florida next week.
2. Susan (bought / buys) a new couch for her apartment before she moved in.
3. Did you (see / have seen) the shooting star in the sky last night?
4. What I (discovered / discover) is that I need to start big projects earlier.
5. My friends and I (walk / walked) to the park yesterday to play catch.

Students write routinely for a range of tasks, purposes, and audiences. Students practice various conventions of standard English.

Name ______________________________

Benchmark Vocabulary

DIRECTIONS Write a sentence using each word.

safeguard fixtures

Write in Response to Reading

Reread pages 144–147 of *A Bright Idea.* Do you agree with the author that using renewable energy sources will make Earth a cleaner and healthier planet? Use details from the text to support your answer. Write your answer below, on a separate sheet of paper, or in a new document.

Students demonstrate contextual understanding of Benchmark Vocabulary. Students read text closely and use text evidence in their written answers.

Name ___________________________

Shaping Tomorrow Through Innovation Today

Suppose you could fast forward to the year 2075. Has the world run out of gasoline and clean water, or has new technology conserved important resources? If we adapt now to energy-efficient lifestyles and products, life in the future will be better than it is today. Many smart changes are already in the works.

To decrease air pollution and gas consumption, cities are encouraging people to ride bicycles. The Boston Bikes program has doubled the number of bicycle riders by adding bike routes and places to park bikes. New York City has announced plans for a bike-share program. After adding 250 miles of bike paths, the city is purchasing bicycles and developing rental stations. However, objections to the location of stations still must be resolved.

Automobile manufacturers are producing electric cars that travel farther between charges, making them a practical replacement for gasoline-powered cars. With a recent invention of lithium-air batteries that use graphene bubbles, a car can go 300 miles on a single charge. In addition, one automaker is planning to introduce laser headlights that will be 1,000 times brighter than LED headlights yet use half the power. The amount of power needed to run the engine is reduced, but will the bright lights be safe? Engineers say yes.

Advances in solar and wind power are reducing our need for limited resources such as coal and oil. The problem with solar energy in the past was that too many panels were needed to collect enough of the sun's energy. Effective use of the sun's power is now possible with flexible solar panels. They can be used for roofs and walls, providing a large surface to collect the sun's power. Patrick Marold's wind turbines, built from refrigerator fan blades and bicycle generators, could make effective use of wind power. Using translucent tubes and LED lights, the generators convert wind into light that glows through the tube and illuminates the ground.

Another promising invention includes a fabric made from milk that feels like silk and is washable. Created by fashion designer Anke Domaske, Qmilch is environmentally friendly because it uses only a half-gallon of water to make 2 pounds of fabric, while more than 10,000 liters of water are needed for 2 pounds of cotton. Changing our lives today will make the year 2075 a wonderful time to be alive.

Students read text closely to determine what the text says.

Name ____________________

Sleuth work

Gather Evidence Circle information in the text that discusses energy-efficient lifestyles. Underline information in the text that discusses energy-efficient products.

Gather Evidence: Extend Your Ideas Why does the author think that we need to adopt energy-efficient lifestyles?

Ask Questions Identify the invention or lifestyle change that interests you most. Then brainstorm one question you have about this invention or lifestyle change.

Ask Questions: Extend Your Ideas How could you apply the product or lifestyle change you find most interesting to your own life?

Make Your Case Put brackets around the invention or lifestyle change you think will have the greatest environmental impact in the future.

Make Your Case: Extend Your Ideas Explain why you think this particular invention or lifestyle change would have the greatest environmental impact.

Students read text closely to determine what the text says.

Name ______________________

Informative/Explanatory Writing: Select and Research a Topic Research one of the planets in our solar system that you would like to write a brochure about. Conduct your research using print and online resources. Make sure all of your sources are reputable and reliable. Take notes about your topic using those sources, and create a reference list of all sources used. Use a separate sheet of paper or start a new document.

Avoid Inappropriate Shifts in Verb Tense

DIRECTIONS Rewrite each sentence, correcting errors in verb tense usage.

1. First I will walk to Jennifer's house, and then we walked to Linda's house and went to school.

____

____

2. Matthew and Daniel will watch a movie together yesterday.

____

____

3. Ellie slept over at her friend's house tomorrow night after watching the school play.

____

____

4. I will run a marathon last year.

____

____

5. Who wanted to earn extra money this weekend by doing some yard work?

____

____

Students write routinely for a range of tasks, purposes, and audiences. Students practice various conventions of standard English.

Name ______________________________

Benchmark Vocabulary

DIRECTIONS Write a sentence using each word.

components reliance complex modifying

____

____

____

____

____

____

____

____

Write in Response to Reading

Reread pages 150–151 of *What Is Coding, Anyway?* How does coding apply to your everyday life? Use details from the text to support your answer. Write your answer below, on a separate sheet of paper, or in a new document.

____

____

____

____

____

____

____

____

____

____

Students demonstrate contextual understanding of Benchmark Vocabulary. Students read text closely and use text evidence in their written answers.

Name ______________________________

Text Structure

DIRECTIONS Using evidence from the text, answer the following questions about page 154 of *What Is Coding, Anyway?*

1. What does the secret message say?

2. How were you able to determine the secret message?

3. How does the code shown relate to programming technology?

4. How does giving a sample code improve your comprehension of the text?

Students analyze and respond to literary and informational text.

Name ____________________

Writing

Informative/Explanatory Writing: Outline Ideas Organize the information from your research in Lesson 13 by creating an outline. Choose or create graphics to support the ideas expressed in your outline. Use a separate sheet of paper or start a new document.

Conventions

Avoid Inappropriate Verb Tense Shifts in Paragraphs

DIRECTIONS Circle the incorrect verb tense shift in each paragraph. Then write the correction on the line below the paragraph.

1. My mom wanted me to text her when I got to Marc's house. It will be a long walk. It took me 45 minutes to get there.

   ____

2. My dad and I are baking a cake for my sister's graduation. It will be delicious! It had strawberry filling and chocolate frosting.

   ____

3. My favorite song came on the radio. I sing along while I listened to it.

   ____

4. I will take my computer to be fixed tomorrow. It will be freezing up all the time.

   ____

5. Mom buys a new serving platter for our family Sunday dinners. I felt bad when I broke it. We only used it one time.

   ____

Students write routinely for a range of tasks, purposes, and audiences. Students practice various conventions of standard English.

Name ____________________

Benchmark Vocabulary

DIRECTIONS Write a sentence using each word.

array sensors translate

____

____

____

____

____

____

Write in Response to Reading

Reread pages 160–164 of *What Is Coding, Anyway?* How does the author relate the topic of coding to his readers, who are mainly middle-school students? Use details from the text to support your answer. Write your answer below, on a separate sheet of paper, or in a new document.

____

____

____

____

____

____

____

____

____

____

Students demonstrate contextual understanding of Benchmark Vocabulary. Students read text closely and use text evidence in their written answers.

Name ______________________________

Writing

Informative/Explanatory Writing: Write a Draft Write a first draft of a brochure about the planet you chose for your research in previous lessons. Use your outline from Lesson 14 as a plan for writing your draft. Use a separate sheet of paper or start a new document.

Conventions

Correcting Sentence Fragments

DIRECTIONS Rewrite each sentence fragment to make a complete sentence.

1. Went to the theater.

____

2. The play we saw.

____

3. Afterwards, we went.

____

4. At Allen's jokes.

____

5. We get to.

____

Students write routinely for a range of tasks, purposes, and audiences. Students practice various conventions of standard English.

Name ______________________________

Benchmark Vocabulary

DIRECTIONS Write a sentence using each word.

customized collaborate compatible

____

____

____

____

____

____

Write in Response to Reading

Reread page 168 of "Coming Soon to a Hospital Near You!" What are some of the advantages that 3D-printed prosthetics have over traditional prosthetics? Use details from the text to support your answer. Write your answer below, on a separate sheet of paper, or in a new document.

____

____

____

____

____

____

____

____

____

____

Students demonstrate contextual understanding of Benchmark Vocabulary. Students read text closely and use text evidence in their written answers.

Name ______________________

Writing

Informative/Explanatory Writing: Review and Revise Review the first draft of your brochure about a planet in our solar system, with a focus on sense and clarity of the text. Make sure to define any unfamiliar vocabulary and to use formal language. Make revisions to the text as needed. Review the graphics you chose to include in the brochure, and write a caption for each graphic. Use a separate sheet of paper or start a new document.

Conventions

Spell Possessive Pronouns Correctly

DIRECTIONS Rewrite each underlined pronoun and spell it correctly.

1. <u>There</u> going to a concert on Friday night.

   ____

2. Are you sure that <u>your</u> supposed to pick me up after school?

   ____

3. The turtle cracked <u>it's</u> shell.

   ____

4. My family went to <u>they're</u> house for dinner.

   ____

5. Can we have a sleepover at <u>you're</u> house this weekend?

   ____

Students write routinely for a range of tasks, purposes, and audiences. Students practice various conventions of standard English.

Name ______________________________

Greek and Latin Roots *astr, sol, arch, dem, geo*

DIRECTIONS Write the meaning of each root and give an example of a word that has that root.

1. astr ____________________

2. sol ____________________

3. arch ____________________

4. dem ____________________

5. geo ____________________

DIRECTIONS Use your knowledge of Greek and Latin roots to match the word with the definition.

6. government without rulers _____ a. endemic

7. native to a certain region _____ b. geopolitics

8. shortest or longest day of year _____ c. anarchy

9. science and technology of space flight _____ d. solstice

10. politics affecting the world _____ e. astronautics

DIRECTIONS Choose words from the following list to complete the sentences. Not every word in this list will be used: *geomagnetic, solarium, astrophysical, archaic, democrat, demography, solarize, geographer, astrology, archetypal.*

11. Frank had to think about writing a science fiction story using different ____________ characters.

12. He wondered if an expert ____________ could play a role in his narrative.

13. The expert could describe the ____________ of the population of imaginary distant planet.

14. Moreover, the character could receive all her powers by occasionally going into a ____________ to recharge her power from the sun's rays.

15. Another character, this time a villain, could enter the picture by using ____________ to predict the influence of the stars on the distant people's lives.

Students apply grade-level word analysis skills.

Name ______________________________

Benchmark Vocabulary

DIRECTIONS Write a sentence using each word.

extraordinary functioning complex

____

____

____

____

____

____

Write in Response to Reading

Reread pages 130–133 of *George's Cosmic Treasure Hunt,* page 140 of *A Bright Idea,* page 161 of *What Is Coding, Anyway?,* and page 170 of "Coming Soon to a Hospital Near You!" Which invention or idea do you think has had, or will have, the greatest impact on people? Use details from the text to support your answer. Write your answer below, on a separate sheet of paper, or in a new document.

____

____

____

____

____

____

____

____

____

____

Students demonstrate contextual understanding of Benchmark Vocabulary. Students read text closely and use text evidence in their written answers.

Name ______________________________

Scientific Language

DIRECTIONS Using evidence from the text, answer the following questions about *George's Cosmic Treasure Hunt, A Bright Idea, What Is Coding, Anyway?,* and "Coming Soon to a Hospital Near You!"

1. Reread pages 143–147 of *George's Cosmic Treasure Hunt*. How did the language used in the story and the informative feature help you to better understand the experience of watching a spacecraft liftoff?

2. Reread page 144 of *A Bright Idea*. What scientific language is used on this page, and how were you able to determine the meanings of these terms?

3. Reread page 160 of *What Is Coding, Anyway?* and page 170 of "Coming Soon to a Hospital Near You!" Compare the difficulty level of the scientific language in these two texts. Was one text easier to understand than the other? Explain your answer.

Students analyze and respond to literary and informational text.

Name ______________________________

Writing

Informative/Explanatory Writing: Edit and Proofread Edit and proofread your brochure about a planet in our solar system, and correct any errors that you may find. It may also be helpful to have a classmate edit your brochure, as they can find errors that you might miss. Use a separate sheet of paper or start a new document.

Conventions

Use Standard English

DIRECTIONS Rewrite each sentence using standard English.

1. I was like upset that I was sick and had to miss the concert.

____

2. We need to leave now OK if we want to arrive on time.

____

3. We don't want to like miss our flight.

____

4. Like I am excited about the new lunch menu at school.

____

5. OK, that was too funny.

____

Students write routinely for a range of tasks, purposes, and audiences. Students practice various conventions of standard English.

Name ______________________________

Benchmark Vocabulary

DIRECTIONS Write a sentence using each word.

components collaborate

____

____

____

____

Write in Response to Reading

Reread the first page of each text in this module: *George's Cosmic Treasure Hunt, A Bright Idea, What Is Coding, Anyway?,* and "Coming Soon to a Hospital Near You!" Compare and contrast how each passage attempts to engage the reader. Use details from the text to support your answer. Write your answer below, on a separate sheet of paper, or in a new document.

____

____

____

____

____

____

____

____

____

____

____

____

Students demonstrate contextual understanding of Benchmark Vocabulary. Students read text closely and use text evidence in their written answers.

Name ____________________

Writing

Informative/Explanatory Writing: Publish and Present Choose the publishing format that best suits your audience and that they will respond positively to. Remember to choose an appropriate font and text colors that will make your brochure easy to read and look professional. Use a separate sheet of paper or start a new document.

Conventions

Use Strategies to Improve Expression

DIRECTIONS Rewrite each sentence to make it more precise, vivid, and interesting.

1. The creek flooded during the storm.

____

____

2. The sun is shining.

____

3. It got cold quickly.

____

4. Everyone should have a weather emergency kit.

____

____

5. The storm rolled over the mountains.

____

____

Students write routinely for a range of tasks, purposes, and audiences. Students practice various conventions of standard English.